Building a Web App with Blazor and ASP .NET Core

Create a Single Page App with Blazor Server and Entity Framework Core

Jignesh Trivedi

FIRST EDITION 2020

Copyright © BPB Publications, India

ISBN: 978-93-89845-457

All Rights Reserved. No part of this publication may be reproduced or distributed in any form or by any means or stored in a database or retrieval system, without the prior written permission of the publisher with the exception to the program listings which may be entered, stored and executed in a computer system, but they can not be reproduced by the means of publication.

LIMITS OF LIABILITY AND DISCLAIMER OF WARRANTY

The information contained in this book is true to correct and the best of author's & publisher's knowledge. The author has made every effort to ensure the accuracy of these publications, but cannot be held responsible for any loss or damage arising from any information in this book.

All trademarks referred to in the book are acknowledged as properties of their respective owners.

Distributors:

BPB PUBLICATIONS
20, Ansari Road, Darya Ganj
New Delhi-110002
Ph: 23254990/23254991

MICRO MEDIA
Shop No. 5, Mahendra Chambers,
150 DN Rd. Next to Capital Cinema,
V.T. (C.S.T.) Station, MUMBAI-400 001
Ph: 22078296/22078297

DECCAN AGENCIES
4-3-329, Bank Street,
Hyderabad-500195
Ph: 24756967/24756400

BPB BOOK CENTRE
376 Old Lajpat Rai Market,
Delhi-110006
Ph: 23861747

Published by Manish Jain for BPB Publications, 20 Ansari Road, Darya Ganj, New Delhi-110002 and Printed by him at Repro India Ltd, Mumbai

Dedicated to

I would like to say many thanks to my mother Mrs Saryuben Trivedi and my wife Mrs Poorvi for their support. They deserve to have their name on the cover as much as I do for all their support made this possible. I would also like to say thanks to all my family members Girish Kumar Trivedi (father), Rakesh and Tejas (brother) for their continuous guidance and support to achieve my goals.

-Jignesh Trivedi

About the Author

Jignesh Trivedi is working as a software developer with a leading organization and having more than 14 years of experience. He is very passionate about Microsoft Technologies. He is an author, speaker, and Microsoft MVP. He loves building great products and POC (proof of concepts) using the best available technologies. He loves to share his knowledge by contributing to the Developer community.

He is awarded as MVP by Microsoft for his exceptional contribution in Microsoft technologies under the category "Developer Technologies" since year 2016. He is also a blogger and author of articles on various technologies. He is also a speaker and delivered talk on various technologies like ASP.NET Core, Angular, MVC etc. in the public events.

About the Reviewer

Tejas Trivedi has over 14 years of industry experience and currently works as a Software Architect for a leading organization. He is technical enthisiastic and his experience in Microsoft technologies raninging from VC++,C++ to his current speciality in .NET with C#, ASP.NET ,Azure Clould , Micro services and DevOps. Tejas has been developing in .NET technologies since .NET was first in beta, and is a Technical architect for software solutions using .NET technology. He is active member, blogger and speaker of various Microsoft communities in India. Tejas is currently focusing on overall architecture, solution design and Microsoft cloud solutions.

Acknowledgement

There are a few people I would like to say thanks for their continued and ongoing support given to me during the writing of this book. First and foremost, I would like to thank my wife for support me as I was spending many weekends and evenings on writing this book. I could have never completed this book without her support. I would like to say thanks to my both brother for their support and guidance.

I would also like to say thanks BPB Publications for giving me this opportunity to write my first book for them and also say thanks to the all team member who are contribute in this book.

Preface

Blazor is a new, open-source, and SPA web framework that allows you to build a web application using C# and HTML. Blazor enables you to write C# code instead of JavaScript.

This book is a comprehensive guide about the new modern Blazor framework. It begins with an introduction to the Blazor and its components and concepts. It explains how you can start the development process, what tools you can use to develop an application, and how you can deploy it. You will then learn more about Data-bind, Event-binding, layout, routing, JavaScript interop, and Dependency Injection. Concepts such as Authentication and authorization, error handling are also covered. Towards the end, you will learn how to deploy your Single Page Application Using Blazor. Over the 10 chapters in this book, you will learn the following:

Chapter 1 explain basic of the Blazor, and the programmer needs to get started with Blazor. Also, explain the Blazor booting process and how component renders in Blazor application.

Chapter 2 explain about the Blazor component, a different way to create the Blazor component, the life cycle of component, and the templated component.

Chapter 3 talk about the basic concept of Blazor, such as data binding, event binding, layouts, routing, and validation.

Chapter 4 discusses about how to inject the service dependency in Blazor application.

Chapter 5 explains how to invoke JavaScript function using the .net code and invoke the .net function from JavaScript.

Chapter 6 talks about state management. Blazor application is a stateful app framework. The user state is held in server memory in the circuit. This chapter addresses state persistence in Blazor server-side apps.

Chapter 7 explains the essentials of authentication & authorization and how can we achieve in Blazor application. It also explains the different ways to do authentication & authorization using third-party services such as Google API, Microsoft and Facebook API.

Chapter 8 describes about handling error and introduction to the logging framework provided by ASP.net core. It also explains about 3rd party logging framework providers.

Chapter 9 explains how to start the development of Blazor server / client project / SPA. This chapter do revision of all preceding chapters.

Chapter 10 explains the hosting and deployment of Blazor server / client application on various platforms such as IIS and Azure.

Downloading the code bundle and coloured images:

Please follow the link to download the
Code Bundle and the *Coloured Images* of the book:

https://rebrand.ly/t83tggi

Errata

We take immense pride in our work at BPB Publications and follow best practices to ensure the accuracy of our content to provide with an indulging reading experience to our subscribers. Our readers are our mirrors, and we use their inputs to reflect and improve upon human errors if any, occurred during the publishing processes involved. To let us maintain the quality and help us reach out to any readers who might be having difficulties due to any unforeseen errors, please write to us at :

errata@bpbonline.com

Your support, suggestions and feedbacks are highly appreciated by the BPB Publications' Family.

Table of Contents

CHAPTER 1
An Introduction to Blazor

Introduction

The Blazor is a new web framework that can run in any browser. Using the Blazor framework, you can create a rich and modern **Single Page Application (SPA)**. It allows us to create both server-side and client-side applications. The server application code runs on the server and communicates with UI by SignalR. The client application runs in the browser on mono via WebAssembly.

In this chapter, we'll cover the following topics

- What is Web Assembly?
- What is Blazor?
- Prerequisite Blazor development
- Features of Blazor
- Blazor supported platforms
- Creating our first Blazor application
- How Blazor application renders in the browser?
- Understand Blazor booting process
- Render tree in Blazor application

- Blazor Client-side
- Blazor Server-side

Objectives

- Understand WebAssembly and Blazor
- Understand the features of Blazor
- Know prerequisite to start Blazor application development
- Know Blazor supported platforms
- Understand the internal working of Blazor application
- Understand the type of Blazor application

What is Web Assembly?

WebAssembly is an open standard and defined a portable binary code format. It was developed at the **World Wide Web Consortium (W3C).** The most modern browser supports the WebAssembly without any plug-in. It is similar to low-level assembly language with a compact binary that runs with a near equal performance provided by native language. It can also run along with JavaScript, and both can work together. It enables you to create high-performance applications on web pages. It is not a replacement for JavaScript. It is also referred to as WASM. Following are some features of WebAssembly:

- Efficient and fast
- Open and debuggable
- Hardware independent
- Language independent
- Platform independent
- Part of the open web platform
- memory-safe

Developers do not write code directly in the WebAssembly but write code in high-level languages such as C#, F#, and so on. The respective language code compiler compiles code into WebAssembly bytecode, and it runs on the client (that is, a web browser) where this translated into native machine code. The execution performance is nearly equal to JavaScript, but there is overhead of downloading the WASM module and setting it up. However, it is a one-time activity. It provides a sandboxed execution model with the same security models that exist for JavaScript. You can call JavaScript function from the WebAssembly module and vice versa.

Currently, WebAssembly runs under a web browser is the most common scenario, but its future is not limited to the web. It may be more useful in mobile apps, desktop apps, and many more.

As the name suggests itself, it is more likely an assembly language that consumed by the machine. Developers cannot write code directly in WebAssembly, but code written in a high-level language, and then it compiledinto WebAssembly. This is done by any of the following three ways:

- **WebAssembly-based interpreter:** In this way, language is not translated into WebAssembly but interpreter for the language written in WebAssembly. Currently, Ruby and Python have interpreters that translated code to WebAssembly.

- **Direct compilation:** Some of the language compilers has the ability to translate source code into WebAssembly. Currently, C/C++, Kotlin/Native, and Rust compiler have a native way to generate WebAssembly.

- **Third-party tools:** If the language does not have native support to generate WebAssembly, you can use a third party tool/utility to convert source code to WebAssembly.

The WebAssembly is not the replacement of the JavaScript. It is designed to work with JavaScript and compatible with other web technologies such as HTML and CSS. The higher-level languages such as C#, VB.net, C++, and so on. can be compiled into WebAssembly that runs under the same browser sandbox environment as JavaScript code is running.

When JavaScript code gets executed, first goes through the process of parsing and compilation, and then, the **Just in Time (JIT)** compiler performs speculative execution of binary code. The WebAssembly modules are compiled in a higher-level language, and they are already parsed and compiled, so they go through a decoding phase before executed by JIT. Typical execution of JavaScript and WebAssembly in browser sandboxas shown in the following *Figure 1.1: JavaScript and WebAssembly execution in Browser sandbox:*

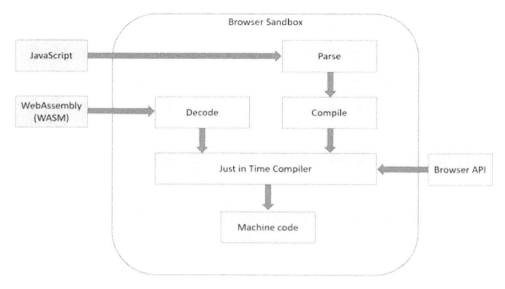

Figure 1.1: JavaScript and WebAssembly execution in Browser sandbox

As you have seen here, both JavaScript and WebAssembly code execution are similar at the JIT compiler.

Security considerations

WebAssembly does not provide full access to the computer environment on that it executed. All the interaction with the environment (such as I/O access, OS Call) can be done by invoking function provided by Embedder. The Embedder can be defined as security policies. The WebAssembly is translated source code to machine code and run on the host hardware, so it is vulnerable for side-channel attacks on hardware. The embedder may have to do something to isolate WebAssembly computations.

WebAssembly limitations

The WebAssembly is very powerful but has a certain limitation:

- The WebAssembly does not have support for direct access to DOM and Browser API.
- The WebAssembly has to rely on JavaScript interop to update the DOM and access the browser API such as SVG, Canvas, and built-in APIs (history, local storage, location, and so on).

- The JavaScript script has its own garbage collection, but WebAssembly does not have a garbage collector. It uses mono GC for the Blazor application.

Facts about WebAssembly

There are a few facts about the WebAssembly listed as follows:

Is WASM kill JavaScript?

No, WASM is not a replacement for JavaScript, but it was created to meet the performance requirement of the web application.

Is WASM a new programming language?

It is not a programming language, but it is the intermediate binary format that works as a compiler for higher-level languages such as C, C++, and rust. The end-goal of WASM had not become a programming language, but it is binary text representation.

Can other programming languages write WASM code other than C and Rust?

The WASM is not a programming language, but it more like the compiler. Many high-level languages such as C# supported by WASM. There are few limitations with WASM that describe previously.

Is it an upgraded version of Silverlight?

No, it is not an upgraded version of Silverlight. The Silverlight required plug-in to run the application on the browser, whereas WebAssembly does not require any plug-in.

These are the facts about the WebAssembly that one must know before they start working with it.

What is Blazor?

Browser + Razor (Blazor) is a new web framework for building **Single Page Application (SPA)** using .NET Core framework that uses Mono WebAssembly runtime.

The Mono is an open-source framework sponsored by Microsoft for implementation of the .NET framework (based on the open standard for C# and **Common Language Runtime (CLR))**. It allows you to write code that runs on cross-platform, targeting macOS, Linux, iOS, Android, and Windows. It provides .NET Standard support and has been compiled to WebAssembly. The Mono runtimes compiled into WebAssembly and using Mono **Intermediate Language (IL),** it loads and executes .NET assemblies. In this way, the .NET works in the browser. This runtime bootstraps by the JavaScript file and download the dlls. This JavaScript also provides access to browser API those required to run code. In short, our code gets compiled to .NET standard dlls, and those are downloaded by the browser and the Mono runtimes compiled to WebAssembly.

Mono runs under WebAssembly in two modes: Interpreted and **Ahead-of-time (AOT).**

Interpreted mode

In interpreted mode, the mono runtime compiled to WebAssembly but not our code (in the form of assembly). The browser loadedour .NET assembly (which is in the form of dlls) and executed by mono runtime. This execution model is very similar to desktop CLR. The desktop CLR uses JIT compilation to make execution faster, but Mono is much closer to the pure interpretation model. *Figure 1.2: interpreted compilation mode* shows the graphical representationof interpreted compilation mode working:

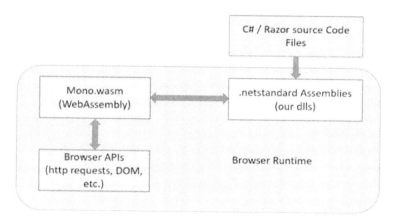

Figure 1.2: interpreted compilation mode

In this model, our .NET assemblies are executed by mono runtime. It results in a performance delay.

Ahead-of-time compiled mode

In this mode, our .NET assemblies are transformed to WebAssembly at build time; hence no interpretation required runtime. The code executes directly as a regular WebAssembly code. This removes unnecessary parsing of .NET assemblies at runtime. It is required to load Mono runtime to use .NET service such as GC (garbage collection). This is very similar to the ngen tool allowed AOT compilation, and CoreRT provides the AOT compilation for .NET core runtime.*Figure 1.3: AOT compiled mode,* shows the graphical representation of AOT compilation mode working:

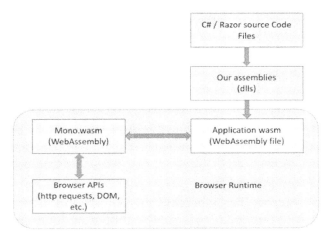

Figure 1.3: *AOTcompiled mode*

The interpreted mode is more useful in faster development where our code gets change, and we can rebuild it using .NET compiler. An AOT compilation takes a long time to build, and it does not save much time in development as may be build frequency is high during development. However, AOT much and more effective in production.

Blazor provides almost all features provided by **Single Page Application (SPA)** such as databinding, routing, and component-based architecture (powered by .NET framework and tooling). It provides a similar development experience as .NET in that you can use the same language for the entire development, and at the same time, it provides a great client framework. The Blazor framework is based on Razor pages that use to create components. This supports dynamic HTML, DOM event, and bindings (both: one-way and two-way). It also provides JavaScript interop, and that allows your C# code and JavaScript can interact with each other. Blazor inspired by top SPA framework such as Angular, React, Vue, and Microsoft UI stacks -Razor pages.

Features of Blazor

Blazor application support most of the features of the SPA provides. It inspires by modern SPA client frameworks such as Angular, Vue, and React. The following are SPA features supported by Blazor:

- **Component-based architecture**: Blazor provides a component-based architecture to develop rich SPA applications. The component is a primary element of the Blazor application. Most of the modern client architecture, such as Angular, provides component-based architecture.

- **Routing**: The client request redirects from one component to another component by using routing. Blazor provides rich routing, and one component can have multiple routes.

- **Layouts**: The layout page provides a common UI element that same across the application, for example, header, navigation, footer, and so on. It helps to remove duplicate code in every page.

- **Data and Event binding**: Data binding is the most powerful feature in software development technologies. Blazor supportsboth one-way / two-way data banding. Data binding providesa bridge between view model (business logic) and view.

- **JavaScript interop**: Blazor access browser API and other functionality using JavaScript interoperability (formally known as JavaScript interop). It also allows calling JavaScript function from our C# code and vice versa.

- **Forms and validation:** Blazor allows to create interactive forms with the handling of user input validation. Blazor is also supporting client-side validation. It also provides server-side events in the component life cycle to handle validation.

- **Dependency injection**: This is the beauty of .NET Core framework;it provides built-in supports of Dependency injection. It allows us to use services by injecting them.

- **Authentication and Authorization**: Blazor server-side allows us to add the functionality of Authentication and Authorization. Blazor provides multiple built-in attributes to achieve authentication. We can also do authentication using third party services such as Facebook, Google, and so on.

- **Multiple Hosing support**: We can host a Blazor application on Azure, IIS, Docker, and so on.

- **Developer friendly features**:
    - *a.* Debugging support in both—browsers and IDE
    - *b.* Rich IntelliSense and tooling
    - *c.* Live reloading in the browser during development when building application

The features listed above make Blazor to powerful development framework. These features are very similar to modern SPA client-side frameworks such as Angular.

Blazor (client) supported platforms

The Blazor application does not require any plug-in to run under the modern browser. Blazor client applications running under browser rely on browser support for WebAssembly. Almost all modern browsers, including Edge, Chrome, Firefox, support WebAssembly. The older browsers are not supported WebAssembly, but still, the Blazor server application can run on these browsers as it does not rely on WebAssembly and all components of Blazor server application executed on the server and event proxied over socket connection (SignalR). *Figure 1.4: Blazor browser support*, shows the list of browser that supports Blazor application:

IE	Edge	Firefox	Chrome	Safari	Opera	Samsung Internet	Blackberry Browser	IOS Safari	UC (Android)
		2 - 45	8 - 50		10 - 37				
6 - 10	12 - 14	46 - 51*	51 - 56*	3.1 - 10.1	38 - 43*	4 - 6.4	7	3.2 - 10.3	
11	15*	52	57 - 75	11 - 12	44 - 60	7.2 - 8.2	10	11 - 12.1	12
	16 - 18	53 - 67	77 - 79	13 - TP	62	9.2		13	
	78	68 - 70							

Not Supported   Supported   * - Not supported by default but need to enabled

Figure 1.4: Blazor browser support

The Blazor application is not run under the older browser, but by using additional polyfills, Blazor application can be run on older browsers such as IE11.

Prerequisite Blazor development

To start development with Blazor, the following two prerequisites must be installed in our machine.

.NET Core Framework (.NET Core SDK)

Blazor application runs on top of the .NET Core framework. It provides a cross-platform solution (working on multiple OS such as Linux, iOS, and Windows).

To develop a Blazor application, you must install .NET Core SDK version 3.0 or above. The recommendation is to use the latest version of .NET core SDK. You can download the latest version of .NET Core SDK from **https://dotnet.microsoft.com/ download.**

Integrated Development Environment - IDE

For the development environment, you have two options: Visual Studio 2019 and Visual Studio Code. If you have a license for Visual Studio, it is recommended to use else you can use Visual Studio community edition. You can download the latest version of Visual Studio (Community/Professional/Enterprise) from **https:// visualstudio.microsoft.com/downloads/.**

Alternatively, you can use Visual Studio Code as IDE. It is a free and cross-platform source code editor developed by Microsoft for Windows, Linux, and iOS. It is a rich source code editor that includes support for debugging, intelligence, code completion, and code refactoring. It has built-in support for source control such as GitHub. It supports a huge number of extensions for different languages and tools. You can download the latest version of the Visual Studio Code from **https://code. visualstudio.com/download.**

It is required to install a couple of extensions. If you want to use Visual Studio Code as an editor, especially C# extension. To install the extension, select the **Extensions** tab from the left side panel and write the extension name in the search box to find the required extension. You must install two extensions: one for C# and another for Razor (Extension name: `Razor+`). Write C# in the search box to find an extension for C# (refer *Figure 1.5: Install C# Extension in Visual Studio Code):*

Figure 1.5: Install C# Extension in Visual Studio Code

Once the C# extension installed, you can install the Razor extension. Write Razor+ in the search box to find an extension for Razor extension in the following screenshot:

Figure 1.6: Install Razor+ Extension in Visual Studio Code

Additionally, you can install Blazor templates if you want to create a Blazor application using **Command Line Interface (CLI).** Using the following command, you can install the Blazor Template from NuGet.

```
> dotnet new -i Microsoft.AspNetCore.Blazor.Templates
```

These templates allow you to create verity Blazor projects such as Blazor library, Blazor stand alone, Blazor client-side. As shown in *Figure 1.7: Blazor templates for dotnet CLI*, CLI list down all available template when you run dotnet new command from the command prompt:

```
MVC ViewImports                                viewimports        [C#]       Web/ASP.NET
MVC ViewStart                                  viewstart          [C#]       Web/ASP.NET
Blazor Server App                              blazorserver       [C#]       Web/Blazor
Blazor (hosted in ASP.NET server)              blazorhosted       [C#]       Web/Blazor/Hosted
Blazor Library                                 blazorlib          [C#]       Web/Blazor/Library
Blazor (Server-side in ASP.NET Core)           blazorserverside   [C#]       Web/Blazor/ServerSide
Blazor (standalone)                            blazor             [C#]       Web/Blazor/Standalone
ASP.NET Core Empty                             web                [C#], F#   Web/Empty
ASP.NET Core Web App (Model-View-Controller)   mvc                [C#], F#   Web/MVC
ASP.NET Core Web App                           webapp             [C#]       Web/MVC/Razor Pages
ASP.NET Core with Angular                      angular            [C#]       Web/MVC/SPA
ASP.NET Core with React.js                     react              [C#]       Web/MVC/SPA
ASP.NET Core with React.js and Redux           reactredux         [C#]       Web/MVC/SPA
Razor Class Library                            razorclasslib      [C#]       Web/Razor/Library/Razor Class Library
ASP.NET Core Web API                           webapi             [C#], F#   Web/WebAPI
```

Figure 1.7: Blazor templates for dotnet CLI

You can use either Visual Studio 2019 or Visual Studio code or CLI to create a Blazor server application. The templates for CLI and Visual Studio can be different.

Creating first Blazor application

The current version of Blazor is only supported for the server application, but you can create a Blazor client application by installing the template. Visual Studio only supports `blazorserverside` template as of now but later on, support multiple templates. If you want to create a Blazor application other than the Blazor server, you can create by .NET CLI.

Creating a project with Visual Studio 2019

To create Blazor application using Visual Studio 2019, open the Visual Studio >> Select **Create New Project** option in the following screenshot:

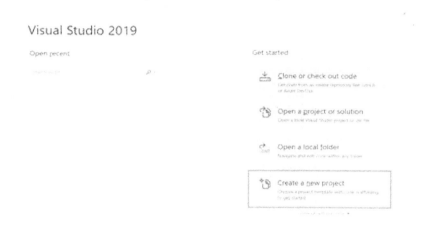

Figure 1.8: Visual Studio new project dialog

Then select **Blazor APP** from the template and then click on **Next** button as shown in the following screenshot:

Figure 1.9: Visual Studio project template selection

Now, you need to fill-up basic information of project such as project and solution name, project location, and whether to create project and solution file created in the same folder as shown in the following screenshot:

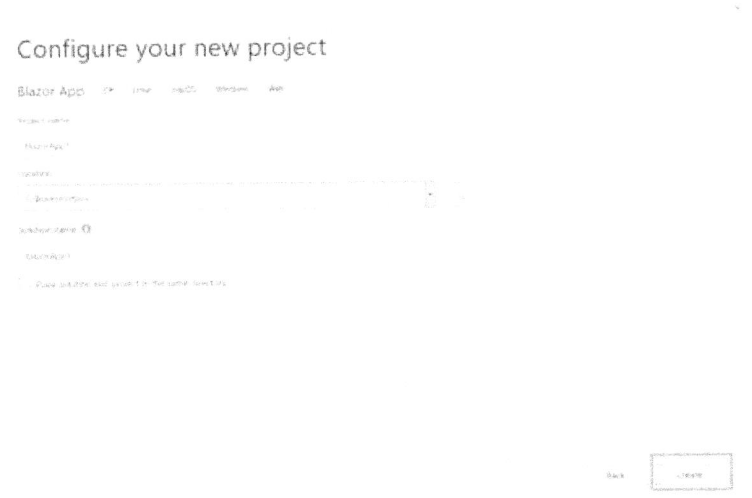

Figure 1.10: Fill basic information about the project

As shown in the following screenshot, you need to select the project template. As describe, currently, Visual studio only supportsthe server app; that is why it shows only one template. Later-on, the Visual Studio development team will add more templates for Blazor application. Now click on **Create** button:

Figure 1.11: Visual studio Blazor Server Template selection

Once you click on the **Create** button, Visual Studio creates a default Blazor server application structure as defined in the template.

Creating a project using dotnet CLI

As described earlier, you can create a Blazor project using dotnet CLI. There are four templates available that allow you to create verity Blazor projects such as Blazor library, Blazor standalone, Blazor client-side *(refer Figure 1.6)*.

The dotnet CLI command can be executed from the Command Prompt / Line. Using the new command, you can createa Blazor project from CLI. Using the following command, you can create a Blazor server application. This will create a new project in the same directory as currently, you are using:

```
> dotnet new blazorserver
```

You can edit the project created using CLI by any of the editors such as VS 2019 or VS code and build / run Blazor application using dotnet CLI commands.

Understand project structure and component

As described earlier, you can create Blazor server-side project using both Visual Studio 2019 and dotnet CLI. When you create a project using a blazorserver template, the Project structure looks as shown in the following screenshot.

The Pages folder contains all the view files with .razor extension. The .razor extension is used for the Blazor component. The `App.razor` is a bootstrap component. The Shared folder contains the layout page. The `_Imports.razor` file contains the common reference of all namespace used by the Blazor component. You will learn more about the Blazor component in later chapters.

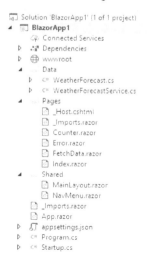

Figure 1.12: Blazor Server project structure

The Blazor template generates server-side code inside Razor pages using `@code` directive. It generates a single file for C# code and Razor code; however, you can create a separate file for view and code file (code behind). The following screenshotshows the code snap of `Counter.cshtml` that generated by the template by default. As you have seen here, the page contains the three parts: routing, UI (HTML + Razor), and C# code (code behind).

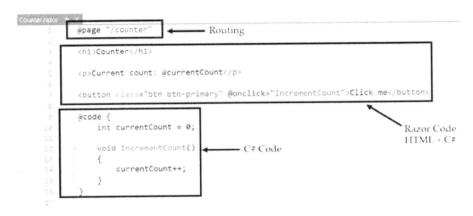

Figure 1.13: Blazor component example

Blazor component may have .cshtml extension. In the next section, you will learn about the booting process of the Blazor application.

Understand Blazor booting process

Blazor is made up of two-part: WebAssembly base .NET runtime and component-based UI. The component of the Blazor app executes on the server on .NET Core, so the entry point for Blazor application is the `Main` method, defined in the `program.cs` file. The following code is for the program.cs file that was generated by the Blazor server template:

```
public class Program
{
    public static void Main(string[] args)
    {
        CreateHostBuilder(args).Build().Run();
    }


    public static IWebAssemblyHostBuilder CreateHostBuilder(string[] args) =>
```

```
BlazorWebAssemblyHost.CreateDefaultBuilder()
        .UseBlazorStartup<Startup>();
}
```

The main method invokes the `CreateHostBuilder` method. This method ensures two things get it done:

- The `BlazorWebAssemblyHost` will call its own CreateDefaultBuilder method
- Call `UseBlazorStartup` method

The `UseBlazorStartup` method accepts the startup class type, where the application is configured. This process is like the ASP.NET Core web application bootup process; only default builder is different. The Startup class may have different name, So `UseBlazorStartup` method accept startup class type. This class has two methods:

1. `ConfigureServices`: The `ConfigureServices` method is not mandatory in startup class. The `ConfigureServices` method is used to configure the service being used in the application.
2. `Configure`:The `Configure` method is used to configure middleware used the application. Using this method, we can control the request pipeline.

To bootup the client side Blazor application, we need to add just the client side app(it is the root component of Blazor application). However, this will may different in the Blazor server application. The following code shows the default implementation of `ConfigureServices` and `Configure` methods in Startup class.

```
public class Startup
{
    public void ConfigureServices(IServiceCollection services)
    {
    }


    public void Configure(IComponentsApplicationBuilder app)
    {
        app.AddComponent<App>("app");
    }
}
```

You can compare the booting of Blazor application with the following figure:

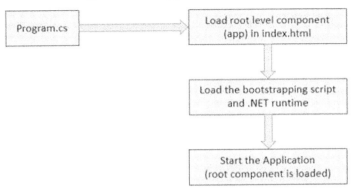

Figure 1.14: Booting Process of Blazor application

Once the Blazor application bootstrapped, the framework generates the render tree for the Blazor component. In the next section, you will learn about how the framework generates a render tree.

Render tree in Blazor application

In the last section, we learned about the booting process of the Blazor application. So, How HTML generate from the Blazor component and render on the browser? This may be the next question in our minds.

Blazor uses JavaScript interop to access the **Document Object Model (DOM)** element, such as input controls, div, span, and so on. The Blazor component is in the form of C# and Razor code, so the first Razor view engine converts it to the dynamic HTML, and then it renders to the browser.

The following figure shows a typical process of accessing DOM by using C# code (Blazor client).

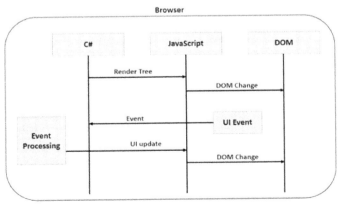

Figure 1.15: Process of accessing DOM by C# - Blazor client

The C# code generates a hierarchical structure of UI components defined in the Razor page. Normally, it refers to a render tree. Using the JavaScript code (`blazor.js`), frameworks rendered the UI structure in browser DOM according to render tree. The JavaScript code then starts to listen to the UI event. When an event is generated by any UI component, it internally invokes the `BrowserRendererEventDispatcher` class to dispatch the event to C#. Then, the event is processed by the C# Code and changes transferred to the UI. The JavaScript code (Blazor) analyzed the changes and applied them to DOM .

The following figure shows the typical process of accessing DOM by using C# code in the Blazor server app.

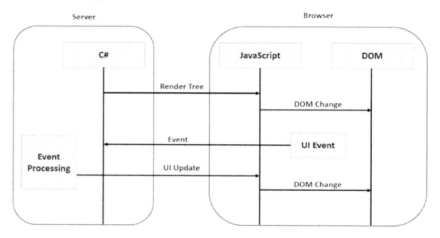

Figure 1.16: Process of accessing DOM by C# - Blazor server

With server-side Blazor, the render tree is built on the server and sentit to the browser using SignalR in serializingform. Blazor JavaScript deserializes the render tree object and updates the DOM. When any event gets triggered by UI, event data gets serialized and then sends it to the server. The .NET code process the render tree, serialized, and send back to the browser.

Blazor client-side

Blazor client-side is a framework for developing a SPA with .NET core framework. It uses WebAssembly and mono runtime to run higher-level language code under browser. WebAssembly is a binary code format for fast downloading and maximum execution speed. It follows open web standards and can be run in the browser without a plug-in.

WebAssembly able to access browser API and DOM using JavaScript interoperability (formally known as **JavaScript interop).** In Blazor client-side application, .NET core code executed via WebAssembly in the browser sandbox with protection that protects client machine against malicious actions. Following *Figure 1.17: Blazor client* shows the typical working structure of Blazor client-side application.

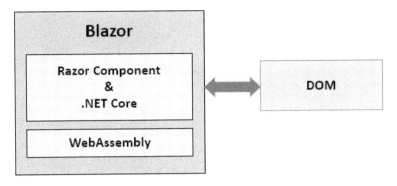

Figure 1.17: Blazor client

When Blazor client-side application builds and runs in browser:

- Higher-level language (C#, F#, and so on) code and Razor files are compiled to .NET assemblies.
- The .NET runtime and assemblies are loaded into the browser.
- Finally, Blazor client-side bootstraps .NET runtime and load assemblies for the application. Using JavaScript interop, Blazor client-side application handles DOM manipulation.

Here, the major concern is a published app (payload) size. It is very critical for the performance factor. The large app size required more time to download to the browser. The Blazor client-side payload must smaller as possible.

Blazor server side

Blazor server-side application is the host on servers in the ASP.NET core application domain. The communication between server and UI is done using SignalR. The SignalR is an open source ASP.NET Core library. It adds supports for real-time web functionality to the web, which enables the server to push content from the server to clients without any delay. The UI sending event from browser to server and server process the request and push back to UI thread running on the browser. The SignalR uses JavaScript interop to handle communication between server and UI.*Figure 1.18: Blazor server shows* a typical working structure of Blazor server-side application:

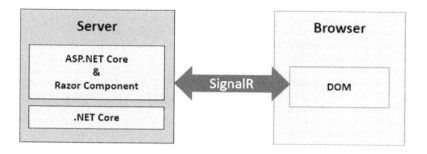

Figure 1.18: Blazor server

The Blazor component renders on the server-side on ASP.NET core and communicates with UI is done using SignalR over the network. In Blazor server-side application does not rely on WebAssembly as components are rendered at the server-side. The Blazor components are run under CoreCLR. This providesa way to run components for client-side Blazor, andthe same component can run on the server.

There are many advantages of Blazor server-side application:

- The app size is smaller; hence app loads faster in the browser.
- The application takes advantage of existing .NET tooling such as debugging and JIT compilation.
- It is not run under mono or WebAssembly, so it can also run on a browser that does not support WebAssembly.
- The UI thread and server communicate with each other using SignalR. It helps to reduce unnecessary page refreshes.

There are also a few drawbacks of Blazor server-side application:

- **Latency of response:** As UI interaction involved using SignalR, so it adds an extra layer of network call.
- **Handle multiple client connections:** Application needs to handle multiple client connections that is also a challenge.
- **No off-line support:** The application stops working when the client network connection goes down.

Blazor server-side and client-side having the same programming structure, but with Blazor server-side, there is no need to send Blazor assemblies and mono runtime to browser to process a render   tree. This is the biggest difference between client-side and server-side app.

Summary

- WebAssembly is developed by W3C, and it is an open standard and defined a portable binary code format. All the modern browser supports WebAssembly
- WebAssembly allows you to create high-performance applications on web pages.
- WebAssembly can run inside the browser without requiringany plug-in
- It is not a replacement of JavaScript
- Blazor = Browser + Razor
- Blazor is a new web framework for building SPA using .NET Core framework
- Blazor supports almost all features that require to develop modernweb application
- You can use Visual Studio 2019 or Visual Studio Code as IDE to develop Blazor application
- You can also create / Build / run a Blazor application using .NET Core CLI. However, it required a template to be install
- Blazor Support both Client-side and Server-side application:
    - **Client-side Blazor:** It uses WebAssembly and mono runtime to run higher-level language code under browser. The major concern with the Blazor client-side is a published app (payload) size.
    - **Server-side Blazor:** Blazor server-side application is the host on server in ASP.NET core application. The communication between server and UI is done using SignalR. It is not used WebAssembly hence app size is smaller compare to Blazor client, and app loads faster in the browser.

What you learned in this chapter?

In this chapter, you have learned about WebAssembly, Blazor, features of Blazor, template and project structure, Blazor supported platforms, and internal working of Blazor application. You also learned how to create a Blazor application and what tool you can use for the development of the Blazor app.

What next?

Blazor supports component-based architecture, and the component is a core part of the Blazor application. In the next chapter, you will learn about the component, different ways to create the component, life cycle methods of component, and templated component.

Questions

1. What is WebAssembly?
2. Is WebAssembly replacement of JavaScript?
3. Is WebAssembly a newer version of Silverlight?
4. What is Blazor?
5. What are the different ways to create a Blazor app?
6. What is the difference between Blazor server-side and client-side app?

CHAPTER 2

Components and Structure for Blazor Applications

Introduction

The component is a core part of Blazor application, and Blazor supports component-based architecture. The component is nothing but similar to the Razor page that contains HTML and C# code. You can refer to the component as a base element of the Blazor application. It means that every views and partial views are components in Blazor. The components may be nested and reused across the projects.

In this chapter, we'll cover the following topics

Following topics are covered:

- What is the Blazor component?
- Create Blazor component
- Life Cycle methods of component
- Component parameters
- Child component
- Templated components
- Cascading values

- Declaring HTML attributes using parameters
- Import components

Objectives

- Understand component and its life cycle methods
- Understand different ways to create the component
- Understand the component parameter
- Understand how to create child component, templated component, and import component
- Understand how to pass the value to cascading component
- Understand how to declare HTML attribute using component parameter

What is the Blazor component?

The componentsare created by using HTML and C# code, just same as the Razor page in ASP.NET Core application. It also refers to the Razor component. The component name must start with uppercase. It has extension either `.razor` or `.cshtml`. The razor component may contain the dynamic rendering logic such as loops and conditional rendering. When the Blazor application is compiled, the C# code and HTML of the component converted into component class. This class name is similar to the name of the component file name.

The @code directive is used to define the member of the component where you can define properties, methods, events, and other component logic. You can also define more than one @code block for the component. Using @ directive, you can define component member that defined in @code block and used for component rendering logic. The component regenerates its render tree when events are triggered. Blazor engine will generate new render tree, compare existing render tree, and applies only the modification to the browser.

You can also include component to another component by declaring them as HTML element syntax. The markup, such as HTML tag and name of the tag is the same as the component name (type). The `@using` statement used to include component namespace that makes components available to use.

Create Blazor component

The component is a core part of the Blazor application, so every page in Blazor application can be considered as a component. The Blazor component consists of C#, CSS, and HTML. There are several ways to create Blazor Components: inline, code behind, and class only.

Using a single file - inline

In this method, HTML markup and C# code are defined in the same file. The C# code is written in the @code block. The markup part contains the Razor syntax (along with C# code) and HTML elements. At the time of compilation, the Blazor engine converts HTML markup and C# code to C# class. Following code shows the example for the inline method of creating component:

```
@page "/routing"


<h1>Page HTML </h1>


@code{
    //C# Code
}
```

This is the default way provided by the Visual Studio template.

Component with code behind

In this method, HTML markup and C# code are in different files. It helps you to separate HTML and C# code rather than both are in the same file. The Razor component must inherit from component code-behind class. Using the @inherit directive, you can inherit components from code behind class. The class must inherit from `Microsoft.AspNetCore.Components.ComponentBase` class. In this method, you can write all C# codes in code behind class, such as to define variables/properties, methods, and events.

The following code shows the example for of method creating component with code behind (`codebehind.cs`).

Your component must inherit from component class (`Codebehind.razor`).

```
@page "/codebehind"
<h3>@Title</h3>
@inherits CodebehindClass
```

Class only component

The Blazor component ends up as a class when complied. Blazor allows you to write component as C# class. This class must inherit from `ComponentBase class.` This base class has method `BuildRenderTree` that renders the component. By adding elements to `RenderTreeBuilder`, you can create a component using C#

code. Using the Layout and `Route` attribute, you can define the layout page and route for the component. The `RenderTreeBuilder` class few methods such as `OpenElement, CloseElement` that helps to add an element to Blazor render tree. Also, the `AddAttribute` method uses to associate the attribute with the element. The `AddContent` method is used to appends a text inside the element.

In the following code example, the h4 and div elements are added to the `BuildRenderTree` and some contents inside the elements the element.

You have seen here, every method, such as `OpenElement` and `AddContent` having a sequence parameter. It indicates the order number of lines in which the Blazor engine renders the HTML defined by code. It is used to generate efficient render tree (refer as diff algorithms) in linear time that much faster than the normally generated render tree using diffalgorithm.

Following code snippet shows how to define component using C# class (`ClassOnly.cs`):

```
namespace Component.Pages
{
    using Component.Shared;
    using Microsoft.AspNetCore.Components;
    using Microsoft.AspNetCore.Components.RenderTree;

    [Route("/classonly")]
    [Layout(typeof(MainLayout))]
    public class ClassOnly : ComponentBase
    {
        private string Text { get; set; } = "My Text";
        protected override void BuildRenderTree(RenderTreeBuilder builder)
        {
            builder.OpenElement(1, "h4");
            builder.AddContent(2, "Class Only Component");
            builder.CloseElement();
            builder.OpenElement(3,"div");
            builder.AddContent(2, Text);
            builder.CloseElement();
        }
    }
}
```

Following *Figure 2.1:* Class only component output, shows how preceding class only component render under the browser and what are the elements are generated:

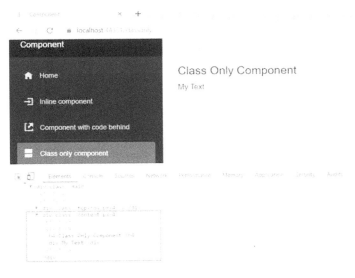

Figure 2.1: Class only component output

The sequence number must be unique within the component. You can also generate sequence numbers programmatically (using increment variable), but you must be more careful when doing this because this will be used for identifying the change in old render tree with newly generated render tree. Based on this difference, Blazor will update UI.

Life Cycle methods of component

The Blazor component is inherited from the `ComponentBase` class. This class contains important life cycle methods that raised when components created, updated, and disposed of. This class contains a life cycle method, and you can override within the component. Both `sync` and `async` methods are available.

The Blazor component has mainly three life cycle events:

- OnInitialized (OnInitializedAsync)
- OnParametersSet (OnParametersSetAsync)
- OnAfterRender (OnAfterRenderAsync)

OnInitialized and OnInitializedAsync

These methods are called when the component has been initialized. The `OnInitialized` event first executed and then `OnInitializedAsync`. Both event fire only onetime in the component life cycle. You can use the OnInitializedAsync event when any asynchronous operations need to perform on component initialization and component re-rendered. Following is the code snippet for defining both the method. You can also use both methods together for one component.

```
protected override void OnInitialized()
{
    ...
}


protected override async Task OnInitializedAsync()
{
    ...
}
```

Once the component is initialized, it starts to receive and bind the parameters from its parent.

OnParametersSet and OnParametersSetAsync

These events are fired after the component initialized, and the component is ready to receive the parameters from its parent. Before this event, parameter values are already assigned to the properties. These events fired every time when updated parameters are received from the parent. Following is the code snippet for defining both the methods:

```
protected override void OnParametersSet()
{
    ...
}


protected override async Task OnParametersSetAsync()
{
    ...
}
```

These methods allow you to modify parameters and rebind with properties.

OnAfterRender and OnAfterRenderAsync

These events are fired after rendering of components finished, and all the references are available to use. This is the best place to write JavaScript interop when using server-side Blazor. The `firstRender` parameter supplied by the framework when the event fired. This parameter is type boolean. It set to true when the component instance is renderedthe first time. This can help you to ensure that initialization work performed once. Following is the code snippet for defining both the methods:

```
protected override void OnAfterRender(bool firstRender)
{
    ...
}


protected override async Task OnAfterRenderAsync(bool firstRenders)
{
    ...
}
```

There are a couple of more methods in `ComponentBase` class those are not part of the component life cycle but very close to life cycle events. These methods are `SetParametersAsync` and `ShouldRender`.

SetParametersAsync

This method triggers before parameters are set. You can modify the parameters before they are rendering to the component. The modified values are not assigned by default. They can be assigned if you call `base.SetParametersAsync` method along with modified parameters. Following is the code snippet for defining `SetParametersAsync` method:

```
public override async Task SetParametersAsync(ParameterView parameters)
{
    //Write your code here to modify parameters

    await base.SetParametersAsync(parameters);
}
```

This event is not part of the component life cycle but very close to the life cycle event. It calls before the component is initialized.

StateHasChanged

It notifies the component when the state has changed, so the component to be re-rendered. This method calls after all life cycle events. You cannot override this method. You can also call this method manually to forcefully re-render component. However, it rarely required to re-render components manually.

Following code snippet shows the example of all life cycle methods as well as supporting methods:

```
@page "/lifecyclemethods"
<h3>Life Cycle Methods</h3>
@code{

    protected override void OnAfterRender(bool firstRenders)
    {
        Console.WriteLine("OnAfterRender");
    }
    protected override async Task OnAfterRenderAsync(bool firstRenders)
    {
        Console.WriteLine("OnAfterRenderAsync");
    }
    protected override void OnInitialized()
    {
        Console.WriteLine("OnInitialized");
    }
    protected override async Task OnInitializedAsync()
    {
        Console.WriteLine("OnInitializedAsync");
    }
    protected override void OnParametersSet()
    {
        Console.WriteLine("OnParametersSet");
    }
    protected override async Task OnParametersSetAsync()
    {
        Console.WriteLine("OnParametersSetAsync");
```

```
    }

    public override async Task SetParametersAsync(ParameterView parame-
ters)
    {
        //Write your code here to modify parameters
        Console.WriteLine("SetParametersAsync");
        await base.SetParametersAsync(parameters);
    }
}
```

When you run the preceding code, you can see sequences of method execution (refer *Figure 2.2: Component lifecycle console output):*

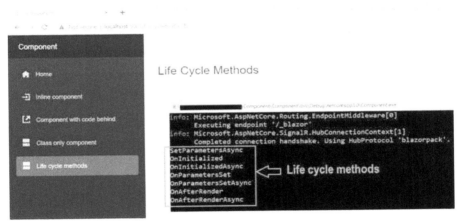

Figure 2.2: Component lifecycle console output

Following *Figure 2.3: Component lifecycle sequence* shows the component life cycle method in sequence.

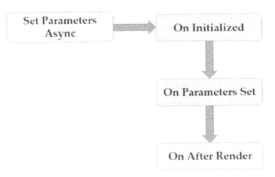

Figure 2.3: Component lifecycle sequence

Dispose component with IDisposable

The component class supports implementingthe Idisposable interface. You can implement an `Idisposable interface using @implements directive.` This interface contains the `Dispose` method. The `Dispose method` is called when the component removed from the UI. Following code snippet shows an example to implement `Idiposable` interface with the component:

```
@implements Idisposable

...

...

@code{

...

...

    public void Dispose()
    {
        Console.WriteLine("Dispose");
    }
}
```

You can invoke code that removes the object from memory in the disposed method, so it helps in memory clean-up and release.

Component parameters

The component may have one or more parameters. Blazor engine automatically binds the value of parameters to properties. To bind component parameters, properties must be defined with public access modifier and decorated with the `Parameter` attribute. The property name must match the parameter name. Following code, snippet shows an example to define the component parameter. As you have seen here, the component `acceptsName` as a parameter and bind with property:

```
@page "/test/{name}"



...

...


@code{
    [Parameter]
```

```
    public string Name { get; set; }

    ...

}
```

You will learn more about the component parameters in the next chapter.

Child component

The component is a core part of the Blazor applicationthat is every page is considered as a component. The component-based architecture is a very famous concept as components are reusable. You can use one component inside another component, generally referred to as a nested component. The inner component generally refers to as a child component. There is no difference between parent component and child component except routing. Child component does not have routing defined as it is always a part of another component, and it may not use as an individual component.

Following is code snippet of child component (`Childcomponent.razor`):

```
<h3>Child Component</h3>

<h5> Your Name: @Name</h5>

@code{
    [Parameter]
    public string Name { get; set; }
}
```

Following is code snippet of parent component (`Parentcomponent.razor`):

```
@page "/parent"
<h3>Parent Component</h3>

<ChildComponent Name="@ChildName" />

@code{
    public string ChildName { get; set; } = "Jignesh";
}
```

As you have seen here, the parent component contains the child component, and its defined HTML element tag and name of the tag is the same as component name (type). When preceding code run, the Blazor engine renders **Child component** inside the **Parent Component** (refer *Figure 2.4: Parent-child component output*).

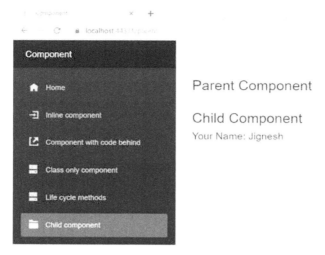

Figure 2.4: Parent-child component output

The parent component may contain one or more child components, and one child component can use inside many components **(Parent Component).**

Templated components

The Templated component is a similar concept as a child component, but it accepts one or more templates as parameters and components render using these parameters. This is very useful to build high-level reusable component. You can also write generic components such as grid view and list view using the templated components.

The templated component defined by using one or more component parameters of `RenderFragment<T>` or RenderFragment. It defined a segment of UI that renders. You can also pass strongly type with RenderFragment parameter that used when render fragment is invoked.

Grid view template example

The following example shows how you can create a generic grid template component. This grid component has three fragments defined: `Header,  Row,  and  Footer`. These fragments are generated using the parameters. The parameter contains the actual HTML and context data, which replaced with a template during the generation of the HTML.

Following is the code snippet of the grid view component `(GridviewTemplate. razor).`

```
@typeparam TItem

<table border="1">
<thead>
<tr>@Header</tr>
</thead>
<tbody>
@foreach (var item in Items)
        {
<tr>@Row(item)</tr>
        }
</tbody>
<tfoot>
<tr>@Footer</tr>
</tfoot>
</table>

@code{
    [Parameter]
    public RenderFragment Header { get; set; }

    [Parameter]
    public RenderFragment<TItem> Row { get; set; }

    [Parameter]
    public RenderFragment Footer { get; set; }

    [Parameter]
    public IReadOnlyList<TItem> Items { get; set; }
}
```

The Grid template component contains three properties (Header, Footer, and Row) of RenderFragment and RenderFragment<t> type and one property (Items) of type IReadOnlyList<T> type. The Items property contains actual data that replaced with the template. The RenderFragment<T> is automatically set by the type of data passed to Items property. You can also define this type using TItem property.

The templated component can be used as a child component in any component. Using the `context` property, you can access data passed to the templated component.

Following code snippet shows how to use grid templated component (`TamplatedComponentExample1.razor`):

```
@page "/extemp1"

@using Component.Model

<h3>Tamplated Component Example</h3>

@if (employees == null)
{
<p><em>Loading...</em></p>
}
else
{
<GridviewTemplate Items="@employees">
<Header>
<th style="width:50px;">ID</th>
<th style="width:100px;">Code</th>
<th style="width:100px;">First Name</th>
<th style="width:100px;">Last Name</th>
</Header>
<Row>
<td>@context.Id</td>
<td>@context.Code</td>
<td>@context.FirstName</td>
<td>@context.LastName</td>
</Row>
<Footer>
<td colspan="4">Total 4 employees</td>
</Footer>
</GridviewTemplate>
}
@code{
```

```
Employee[] employees;

protected override void OnInitialized()

{
    employees = new Employee[3];

    employees[0] = new Employee { Id = 1, Code = "E001", FirstName =
"Jignesh", LastName = "Trivedi" };

    employees[1] = new Employee { Id = 2, Code = "E002", FirstName =
"Rakesh", LastName = "Trivedi" };

    employees[2] = new Employee { Id = 3, Code = "E003", FirstName =
"Tejas", LastName = "Trivedi" };

}

}
```

When you run the preceding code, it generates the grid view (refer *Figure 2.5: Grid view example using Templated component*).

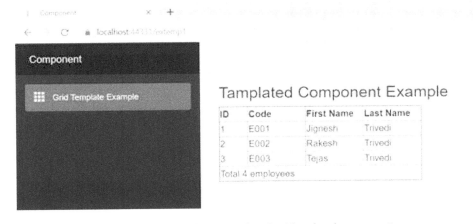

Figure 2.5: Grid view example using Templated component

This example covers the grid view, but you can any kind of templated component based on your requirement.

List view template example

The following example shows how you can create a generic list template component. It defines in a generic way, so use the @typeparam directive to specify type parameters. This component has only one fragment defined (ItemTemplate) of type RenderFragment<T> and one property (Items) of type IReadOnlyList<T> type. The Items property contains actual data that replaced with the template.

Following is the code snippet of list view component (`ListviewTemplate.razor`):

```
@typeparam TItem

@foreach (var item in Items)
{
@ItemTemplate(item)
}

@code{
    [Parameter]
    public RenderFragment<TItem> ItemTemplate { get; set; }
    [Parameter]
    public IReadOnlyList<TItem> Items { get; set; }
}
```

Following code snippet shows how to use list view templated component (`TamplatedComponentExample2.razor`):

```
@page "/extemp2"

@using Component.Model

<h3>Tamplated Component Example</h3>

@if (employees == null)
{
<p><em>Loading...</em></p>
}
else
{
<ui>
<ListviewTemplate Items="@employees" TItem="Employee">
<ItemTemplate>
<li>
@context.LastName, @context.FirstName
</li>
</ItemTemplate>
```

```
</ListviewTemplate>
</ui>
}
@code{
    Employee[] employees;
    protected override void OnInitialized()
    {
        employees = new Employee[3];
        employees[0] = new Employee { Id = 1, Code = "E001", FirstName =
"Jignesh", LastName = "Trivedi" };
        employees[1] = new Employee { Id = 2, Code = "E002", FirstName =
"Rakesh", LastName = "Trivedi" };
        employees[2] = new Employee { Id = 3, Code = "E003", FirstName =
"Tejas", LastName = "Trivedi" };
    }
}
```

When you run the preceding code, it generates the list view (refer *Figure 2.6: List view example using Templated component*).

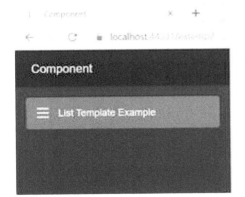

Figure 2.6: List view example using Templated component

Apart from this, you can also define templated components inline when there is only one instance of component usage. You will learn how to define templated components inline in the next section.

Define template inline - using Razor template syntax

You can also use Razor template syntax to define `RenderFragment` and `Render Fragment<T>` values. Following example shows how to define the `RenderFragment` section within the component.

Following is code snippet of templated component define inline (`Tamplated ComponentExample3.razor`):

```
@page "/extemp3"

@using Component.Model

<h3>Tamplated Component Example</h3>

@if (employees == null)
{
<p><em>Loading...</em></p>
}
else
{
@template
<ul>
@foreach (var employee in employees)
        {
@ItemTemplate(employee)
        }
</ul>
}
@code{
    Employee[] employees;
    public RenderFragment template =@<p>Employee List</p>;
    public RenderFragment<Employee> ItemTemplate = (item) =>@<li>@item.
FirstName.</li>;
    protected override void OnInitialized()
    {
```

```
        employees = new Employee[3];
        employees[0] = new Employee { Id = 1, Code = "E001", FirstName =
"Jignesh", LastName = "Trivedi" };
        employees[1] = new Employee { Id = 2, Code = "E002", FirstName =
"Rakesh", LastName = "Trivedi" };
        employees[2] = new Employee { Id = 3, Code = "E003", FirstName =
"Tejas", LastName = "Trivedi" };
    }
}
```

When you run the preceding code, it generates the list view (refer *Figure 2.7: Define templated component inline*).

Figure 2.7: Define templated component inline

The templated component is very useful to create a reusable component that is generic in use.

Cascading values

Sometimes, you need to pass data from the parent component to all its child components. It is possible with the `CascadingValue` element and `Cascading Parameter`. It is very useful when the parameter value needs to set for several component layers. The cascading values and parameters pass the value to all child components from its parent.

The following code snippet shows how to use the `CascadingValue` element in the parent component. Here, the `parentData` value to flow down the component hierarchy, so all the child component can access this value:

```
@page "/cascad"

<h3>Parent Component</h3>
```

```
<CascadingValue Value="@parentData">
<ChildComponent/>
</CascadingValue>

@code{
    private string parentData { get; set; } = "Test Cascading Value";
}
```

The following code snippet shows how can you get use to cascading value using the parameter in child component:

```
<h3>Child Component</h3>

Value: @parentData
@code{
    [CascadingParameter]
    public string parentData { get; set; }
}
```

If you define the `CascadingValue` element in the layout page to share the property value than you can use casecading parameter value to all components which are use same layout page. For example, you can define the theme class at the layout page, and it available to use for all components.

You can also cascade multiple values within the same sub-tree. However, you need to provide a unique name to each `CascadingValue` component and its corresponding `CascadingParameter`.

Following code snippet shows example of defining multiple cascading value elements:

```
@page "/cascad"
<h3>Parent Component</h3>

<CascadingValue Value="@parentData" Name="CascadingValue1">
<CascadingValue Value="@parentData1" Name="CascadingValue2">
<ChildComponent />
</CascadingValue>
</CascadingValue>
@code{
```

```
    private string parentData { get; set; } = "Test Cascading Value";

    private int parentData1 { get; set; } = 100;

}
```

Following code snippet shows how to retrieve cascading parameter value when multiple cascading value elements defined in the parent:

```
<h3>Child Component</h3>

Value : @parentData - @parentData1

@code{

    [CascadingParameter(Name = "CascadingValue1")]

    public string parentData { get; set; }

    [CascadingParameter(Name = "CascadingValue2")]

    public int parentData1 { get; set; }

}
```

You can define the `CascadingValue` element as many as you want, but the name of the parameter must be unique.

Declaring HTML attributes using parameters

You can capture and render additional attributes of HTML elements using the component parameter. The additional attributes must be defined as a dictionary and using the `@attributes` directive, and it can be assigned to the element when the component is rendered. The `@attributes` directive is a Razor directive. This style of defining attribute for HTML elements is very useful when multiple HTML elements are having the same kind of attributes defined and required variety of customizations. This concept is also known as attribute splatting.

In the following example, the first input element uses individual attributes, and the second input element use attribute splatting. As you have seen here, both generate similar HTML when rendered. The parameter must implement `IEnumerable<KeyValuePair<string, object>>` where key as attribute name and value is value for the attribute. You can also use `IReadOnlyDictionary<string, object>` to define attribute splatting:

```
<input id="parameter1" maxlength="10" placeholder="Enter the value"
                required="required" size="40" />

<input id="parameter2" @attributes="MyAttributes" />
```

```
@code{
    [Parameter]
    public Dictionary<string, object> MyAttributes { get; set; } =
        new Dictionary<string, object>()
        {
            { "maxlength", "10" },
            { "placeholder", "Enter the value" },
            { "required", "required" },
            { "size", "40" }
        };
}
```

When you run the preceding code and inspect the generate HTML elements, you can see both input elements having the same kind of HTML.

Figure 2.8: Attribute splatting

In addition, you can also define a parameter with `CaptureUnmatchedValues` property set to true that allows the parameter to match all attributes which do not match with any other parameter.

```
[Parameter(CaptureUnmatchedValues = true)]
public Dictionary<string, object> MyAttributes { get; set; } =
    new Dictionary<string, object>()
    {
        { "maxlength", "10" },
        { "placeholder", "Enter the value" },
        { "required", "required" },
```

```
        { "size", "40" }
};
```

You can define only one parameter with `CaptureUnmatchedValues`.

Import components

Import component is nothing but using one component as a child in another component. You have seen an example in the preceding section to use the component as a child in another component, but both the components are placed in the same location so, it does not require to import child component namespace. The namespace of the component determined by project root namespace and the location of the component. For example, the project's root namespace is `Component,` and it is located under the Shared folder, so namespace for component `Component.Shared`. You can import the namespace of the component to another component using the `@using` directive:

`@using Component.Shared`

You can also import the component in `_imports.razor` file if it is in almost all components.

Summary

- Blazor supports component-based architecture, and the component is a core part of Blazor application
- The component is a simple Razor page that contains HTML and C# code
- It has extension either .razor or .cshtml
- It may contain the dynamic rendering logic such as loops conditional rendering and so on
- There are several ways to create Blazor components:
  - **Inline method:** HTML markup and C# code are in the same file. This is the default way provided by the Visual Studio template.
  - **With code behind**: HTML markup and C# code arein different files. It helps you to separate HTML, and C# code rather than both are in same. The component must inherit from component class, and code behind class must inherit from `ComponentBase class`.
  - **Class only:** There is no view file (no razor component file). All the HTML generated by using C# code.
- The Blazor component has mainly three life cycle events: OnInitialized (`OnInitializedAsync`), OnParametersSet (`OnParametersSetAsync`) and OnAfterRender (`OnAfterRenderAsync`). It supports both sync and async methods:

o **OnInitialized (OnInitializedAsync):** These methods called when the component has been initialized. The OnInitialized event first executed and then execute OnInitializedAsync.

o **OnParametersSet (OnParametersSetAsync):** These events are fired when the component is initialized, and the component also ready receive the parameters from its parent.

o **OnAfterRender (OnAfterRenderAsync):** These events are fired after rendering of component finished. The component and element references are populated when these events fired.

- Apart from these main events, the Blazor component couple of more methods but those are not part of the components life cycle, but they are very close to the life cycle event. These methods are `SetParametersAsync` and `ShouldRender`.

- You can implement the `IDisposable interface` and definethe `Dispose` method. It is called when the component removed from the UI.

- The component may have parameters that bind automatically with properties. However, the property name must match the parameter name.

- You can also put the component inside another component. The inner component generally refers to a a child component.

- The Templated component is a component that accepts one or more templates as parameters and components render using these parameters. It is very useful to build high-level reusable component. Using the templated component, you can write a generic component, such as a gridview and listview.

- Using the `CascadingValue` element and `CascadingParameter`, you pass the parameter value from the parent component to all its child components.

- Using the `@attributes` directive, you can capture and render additional attributes in the HTML element using the parameter. This concept is also known as **attribute splatting**.

What you learned in this chapter?

In this chapter, you learned about the Blazor component, ways to create the Blazor component, and the life cycle event of component. Apart from this, you had learned about the child component, templated component, and how to cascading the value to all child components from the parent.

What next?

In the next chapter, you will be learned about the basic concepts of Blazor, such as data binding, event binding, layout, routing, forms, and validation.

Questions

1. Explain about the Blazor component?

2. What are the different ways to create a Blazor component?

3. Explain different life cycle methods of the Blazor component?

4. What is the use of the SetParametersAsync method? Is it part of the component life cycle event?

5. How can you pass the parameter to the component?

6. What is the child component, and how to import child components?

7. What is the templated component, and what is the use of it?

8. Can we define HTML attributes using component parameters?

CHAPTER 3
Blazor Concepts

Introduction

In the previous chapters, you learned about the basics of Blazor. The Blazor framework allows us to write C# code for the client-side application. Blazor concepts such as data-bind, layout, routing, validation, and so on, are the same for Blazor client-side and server-side applications. In this chapter, you will learn about the Blazor concept: Data and Event Binding, Layouts, routing, and forms and validation.

In this chapter, we'll cover the following topics

- Data binding
  - o One-way data binding
  - o Two-way data binding
- Event Binding
  - o Event Callback
- Layouts
  - o Specify a layout in a component
  - o Define layout globally
  - o Nested layouts

- Routing
    - o @page directive/route attribute
    - o Route parameters
    - o Route constraints
    - o Programmatically navigate one component to another component
    - o Query parameters
- Forms and validation
    - o Data annotations

Objectives

- Understand the basic concepts of Blazor such as Data/Event bind, layout, routing, form, and validation.

Data Binding

Data binding is the most powerful feature of modern web applications. Data binding is a bridge between your view (UI) and ViewModel (business logic). Blazor is providing precious data binding capabilities Which are very similar to the modern client frameworks, such as Angular. ASP.NET Core(Razor) similarly provides one-way and two-way data bindings.

One-way data binding

It is also referred to as interpolation in some of the client frameworks such as Angular. The one-way binding allows you to bind the value of variables/properties to the HTML element in DOM. It is very similar to Razor provide data biding. It is not bound to change the value from UI to your view model.

To do the one-way binding in Blazor, you need to add @ prefix to variable/property name that you want to bind and assign it to the appropriate property of the HTML element.

Following code snippet shows the example of one-way binding:

```
@page /databinding

<h3>Data binding example:</h3>

<h4>One-way binding</h4>

<p>
    @myText
```

```
</p>

@code {
    string myText = This is my test string for one-way binding!;
}
```

In preceding code, `myText` variable used in HTML. When you run this code, `myText` variable value populate under <p> element (refer *Figure 3.1: One-way databinding example):*

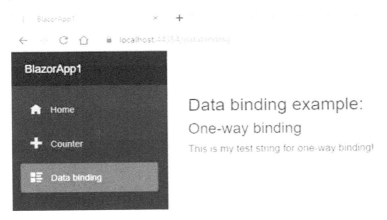

Figure 3.1: One-way databinding example

The one-way binding only allows you to bind variable/property value to the HTML element. The other-side data binding (HTML element to variable/property binding) would not happen in one-way binding.

Two-way data binding

The two-way binding allows you to bind the value of variables/properties to HTML elements in DOM and vice-versa. The two-way binding is achieved by `@bind` directive. This attribute used for both components class and DOM elements in Razor syntax.

In the following code example, the string and bool type properties are bind with textbox and checkbox, respectively. The `@bind` directive bind changed value back to variable/property when appropriate element event (default event) raised. For example, textbox value copied to the variable/property when lost focus event occurs and checkbox value copied on click event:

```
@page /databinding

<h3>Data binding example:</h3>
```

```
<br />

<h4>Two-way binding</h4>
Enter your name:
    <input type=text @bind=Name />
<br />
Have you visited India?
    <input type=checkbox @bind=IsVisited />
<br />

<p><b>Summary</b></p>
You have entered: @Name
<br />
Visited India?: @(IsVisited ? Yes : No)

@code {
    public string Name { get; set; }
    public bool IsVisited { get; set; }
}
```

In the above code, UI gets updated when property/variable value changes from background process and refill property/variable value from UI when the user changes its value (refer *Figure 3.2: Two-way databinding example):*

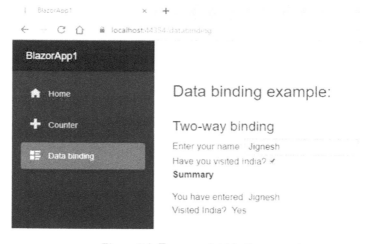

Figure 3.2: Two-way databinding example

With `@bind` attribute, the changes are not reflected immediately; however, this is not true for every element. When the component is rendered, the variable/property value assigned to the input element. As you have seen in the preceding example, textbox value change is not reflected immediately but reflected on lost focus. When you use `@bind` attribute with a textbox, It equivalent to the following code. The onchange event of the textbox is automatically bound to track the changes.

```
<input type=text value=@Name
@onchange=@((UIChangeEventArgs __e) => Name = __e.Value)/>
```

In summary, the property/variable used with `@bind` directive is associated with the value attribute of the HTML element and handles changes using the registered event handler.

As you have seen here, the changes are not getting reflected immediately with `@bind` directive, but value gets reflected when fired register event. Alternatively, you can use the `@bind-value` directive with the event parameter (`@bind-value:event`). Here, you can bind any event and value of variable/property to get an update on the specified event. In the following example code, Value property binds to `oninput` event.

```
...
<input type=text @bind-value=Value @bind-value:event=oninput />
...
@code {
    ...
    ...
    public string Value { get; set; }
    ...
}
```

The `oninput` event fires when the value of the textbox is changing; it is not like onchange that fire on the lost focus of the element. When you run the above code, the value of variable/property gets reflected immediately.

The `@bind` directive also supports for culture parameter (example, `@bind:culture`) that provides `System.Globalization.CultureInfo` for parsing and formatting a value before binding to HTML element.

In following example, double value bind to input element and pass `de-DE` (German) culture, so Blazor will bind `12,34` instead of `12.34` to input element.

```
...
```

```
Number Value Check: <input @bind=doubleValue @bind:culture=culture />
...


@code {

    ...

    ...

    public double doubleValue { get; set; } = 12.34;

    public System.Globalization.CultureInfo culture = new System.Global-
ization.CultureInfo(de-DE);

    ...

}
```

You can also format data to the required format using @bind:format directive. This directive only works with the DateTime data type of variable/property. It is not working with another data type, such as double. With this attribute, you must specify the date format to apply. The specified format is also used to parse date value when an onchange event fired. The @bind:format supports the following .NET data types:

- System.DateTime
- System.DateTimeOffset
- System.DateTime?
- System.DateTimeOffset?

In the following example, JoiningDate property value bind with an input element, and dd-MM-yyyy format is specified:

```
@page /databinding


<h4>Format strings Example</h4>


Joining Date: <input @bind=JoiningDate @bind:format=dd-MM-yyyy />



@code {


    public DateTime JoiningDate { get; set; } = new DateTime(2019,3,23);
}
```

As you have seen here, the date gets formatted in the **dd-MM-yyyy** format before it binds to the HTML element (refer *Figure 3.3: Two-way databinding: date format example*):

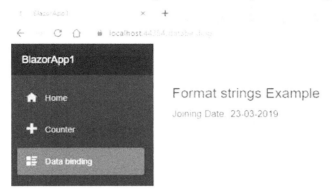

Figure 3.3: Two-way databinding: the date format example

This directive also formats input value back to system format when it binds to variable/property.

Event Binding

Blazor components provide productive event handling. You can register the event of any HTML element using **@on{event}** directive. Here, the event is the name of the event supported by the HTML element, for example, click, submit. This attribute accepts a delegate-type value, and the Blazor component binds attribute value as the event handler.

You can also define event handle as asynchronous that return **Task**. Now, there is no need to update UI manually by calling the **StateHasChanged** method as it is internally handled by Blazor framework.

In the following code example, the button click event has been registered using **@onclick** directive, and checkbox change event has been registered using **@onchange** directive:

```
@page /eventhandling

<h3>Event handling</h3>

<h4>Handle click event of button</h4>

<br />

<button class=btn btn-primary @onclick=IncrementCount>Increment Count</button>

Current Counter: @currentCount
```

```
<hr />
<h4>Handle Check change event of Checkbox</h4>
<br />
Visited India? <input type=checkbox @onchange=handleCheckChange />

Checkbox checked?: @(chkItem ? Yes : No)

@code {
    int currentCount = 0;
    bool chkItem = false;

    void IncrementCount()
    {
        currentCount++;
    }

    private async Task handleCheckChange()
    {
        chkItem = !chkItem;
    }
}
```

The registered events are fired when button clicked and checkbox check change (refer *Figure 3.4: Event databinding*):

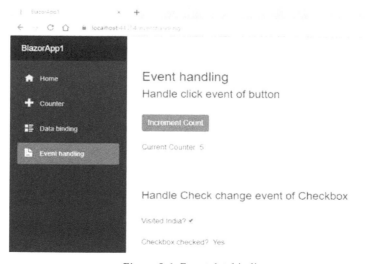

Figure 3.4: Event databinding

The event arguments are also allowed for some events. It is not mandatory to define the event argument in the method definition. You can define an event argument in the method definition. If you need information from it. The following events are supported by UIEventArgs.

Event	Argument class type
Change (for all input element)	UIChangeEventArgs
Keyboard	UIKeyboardEventArgs
Mouse	UIMouseEventArgs
Mouse wheel	UIWheelEventArgs
Mouse pointer	UIPointerEventArgs
Progress	UIProgressEventArgs
Touch	UITouchEventArgs
Focus	UIFocusEventArgs
Error	UIErrorEventArgs
Clipboard	UIClipboardEventArgs
Drag	UIDragEventArgs

Table 3.1: Supported events

You can also define inline method definition (with HTML element) using lambda expression. It is useful when you want to perform small operation. It is not recommended to use everywhere as it may be complex in some scenarios.

```
<button class=btn btn-primary @onclick=@(e=> currentCount++)>Increment
Count</button>
```

In the above code, click event for the button is defined inline using a lambda expression.

Event Callback

Blazor also supports the nested component. The most common scenario in the nested component is that the child component event needs to handle from the parent component method. EventCallback helps you to expose the event across components. You can assign the child component's event callback from the parent component.

Both EventCallback and EventCallback<T> permit asynchronous delegates. The EventCallback structure provides weakly typed. Hence it allows any argument type, but EventCallback<T> is strongly typed, so it required specific argument type.

In the following example, the child component button's onclick event handler passes from the parent component using the `EventCallback` delegate.

Following code snippet shows code for child component (`ChildComponent.razor`):

```
<h3>Child Component</h3>

<button @onclick=OnButtonClick>Click Me(child component)</button>

@code {
    [Parameter]
    public EventCallback OnButtonClick { get; set; }
}
```

Following code snippet shows code for child component (`ParentComponent.razor`):

```
@page /eventcallback
<h3>Parent Component</h3>

<h4>Handle Child Component event in parent Component</h4>
<br />
<ChildComponent OnButtonClick=ShowMessage />
<hr />

<p><b>@message</b></p>

@code {
    private string message;
    private void ShowMessage()
    {
        message = Event: Child component button click!!!;
    }
}
```

When you click to button element of child component, event delegates defined in the parent is fired (refer *Figure 3.5: Event callback example*).

Figure 3.5: Event callback example

The EventCallback is also allowed in multiple nested components.

Layouts

Every application has consistent look and feel throughout the application. Some of the parts of pages such as header, footer, navigation, and copy-right text remain the same on every page. It may result, you need to write duplicate code in every page. The layout page helps you to prevent write duplicate code so, contains common UI parts. Blazor supports layouts that resolved the duplicate code problem. The concept of Layout nearly the same as Master-page in ASP.NET Application. The application may contain multiple layouts. It is also a possible different page may have different layout page.

Introduction to Layouts page

Blazor supports component-based architecture, so every part of the application in Blazor is a component. The Layout page is also one of the components in the Blazor app. It may contain C# / Razor code, databinding, and so on.

Following are the characteristics of the Layout page in Blazor application:

- It inherits from LayoutComponetBase class that contains Body property for renders the content inside the layout.
- @Body directive used to specify the location where the content of the component is rendered.

Following is a code sample of **Layout** page (MainLayout.razor):

```
@inherits LayoutComponentBase

<div class=sidebar>
```

```
    <NavMenu />
</div>

<div class=main>
    <div class=top-row px-4>
        <a href=https://docs.microsoft.com/en-us/aspnet/ target=_
blank>About</a>
    </div>

    <div class=content px-4>
        @Body
    </div>
</div>
```

Typically, the layout looks as following defined by preceding code. Header and left navigation menu are the part of the layout:

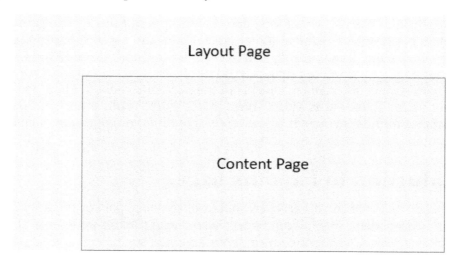

Figure 3.6: Layout page

The content of the component is rendered under the location of the layout page where @Body directive is specified.

Specify a layout in a component

Using the @layout directive, you can define the layout page for the component. The Layout attribute is also available, and it can be applied to the class-based component to define layout.

Example: Using @layout directive:

```
@layout MainLayout
@page /

<h1>Hello, world!</h1>
```

Example: using Layout attribute

```
[Route(/classonly)]
[Layout(typeof(MainLayout))]
public class ClassbasedComponent : ComponentBase
{
    public string Title { get; set; } = Component created by using Class;
    protected override void BuildRenderTree(RenderTreeBuilder builder)
    {
        ...
        ...
    }
}
```

The above-defined method can be used to define the layout page for an individual component. Still, you can also define layout globally that automatically get applied to all the components. You will learn about this in the next section.

Define layout globally

In the Blazor application structure, every folder can optionally contain a file with name _Imports.razor. Whatever directives defined in this file get applied to all Razor pages (component) under located in the same folder structure when application compiled. When directives defined in the root level file, the directives get applied to every Razor page in the application. This file can be used to define the current layout page, so you aren't required to define it in every component. The layout page defined in this file applied to all Razor pages in the folder hierarchy. It is very similar to _ViewImports.cshtml in ASP.NET core. You can also define the namespaces in this file that used in all the views.

Example: _Imports.rozor

```
@layout MainLayout
```

Nested layouts

Blazor supports the nested layouts. It means that a component reference layout page that also refers to another layout page. This feature is useful when you want to create a multi-level structure.

Example

In the following code example, the master layout page (MainLayout.razor) contains the header and left navigation, and another layout page (Layout2.razor) contains only the header part. The MainLayout page is layout page for Layout page 2, and Layout page 2 is the layout for the component.

Layout2.razor:

```
@layout MainLayout
@inherits LayoutComponentBase

<div class=main>
    <div class=px-4>
        <div class=col-md-8 top-row2> Layout page 2 </div>
    </div>

    <div class=content px-4>
        @Body
    </div>
</div>


NestedlayoutExample.razor:
@layout Layout2
@page /nested
<h3>Nested layout Example</h3>

@code {

}
```

Typically, the layout looks as following defined by preceding code:

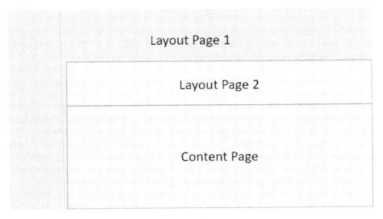

Figure 3.7: Nested Layout page

The layout page is treated as a component in the Blazor application. Typically, it is working as a parent component but in a different manner.

Routing

The URL pattern refers to a route, and the URL pattern matching process is referred to as routing. The routing monitors the requests and decides which component needs to load. Blazor provides a similar kind of routing as ASP.NET Core provides. All the routes defined in the app are configured when the app starts. The routing generates the URL by using route information and map it to endpoint selectors.

As discussed in the preceding chapter, the Blazor server uses `SignalR` for communication between server and UI. To allows the incoming request, it is necessary to map the `SignalR` hub to the default path. So, you should configure endpoints with `MapBlazorHub` method in configure method of startup class (refer following code snippet):

```
public void Configure(IApplicationBuilder app, IWebHostEnvironment env)
{
    ...
    ...


    app.UseRouting();

    app.UseEndpoints(endpoints =>
    {
```

```
        endpoints.MapBlazorHub<App>(selector: app);

        endpoints.MapFallbackToPage(/_Host);

    });

}
```

Blazor engine requires assembly that contains the routing information when the app is initializing. Following code, snippet shows how to configure the router in Blazor. Internally, it finds all defined routes from the app. The default route for the Blazor server application is defined in _Host.razor (that is, @page /):

For Blazor server app:

```
<Router AppAssembly=typeof(Startup).Assembly />
```

For Blazor client app:

```
<Router AppAssembly=typeof(Program).Assembly />
```

@page directive/route attribute

You can define routing for the page using @page directive. When razor page compiles, it generates a route attribute for which @page directive defines and specifies the route template. When the request is processed by the Blazor engine, the route is found into the component classes with route attribute that matches the route template and renders the component if match with the template. You can also define the route using route attribute when component defined as a class.

Example: @page directive

```
@page /simplerouting
<h3>Simple Routing Example</h3>


Example: Route attribute
[Route(/simplerouting )]
[Layout(typeof(MainLayout))]
public class ClassbasedComponent : ComponentBase
{
    …

    …

}
```

You can also define multiple route templates for a single component. The component responds to all the define routes:

Example

```
@page /firstrouting
@page /secondrouting
<h3>Simple Routing Example</h3>
```

The router component allows you to specify a custom error message when a route is not found for the requested route. To set custom route not found message, you need to define NotFoundContent element of router element in App.razor file (refer following code in App.razor):

```
<CascadingAuthenticationState>
    <Router AppAssembly=typeof(Startup).Assembly>
        <NotFoundContent>
            <p>Sorry, there's nothing at this address.</p>
        </NotFoundContent>
    </Router>
</CascadingAuthenticationState>
```

When the route is not found, the Blazor engine will show the custom error message that you have defined (refer *Figure 3.8: NotFoundContent output*):

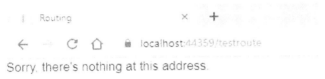

Figure 3.8: NotFoundContent output

When the component with @page directive is compiled, the Blazor engine generates a class component with a route attribute.

Route parameters

The route may have a route parameter. The route parameters are the value that passed with a route. Using parameters, you can pass data that can be accessed when component initializes. It is defined using curly braces ({}) in the routing template with @page directive or route attribute. The route parameters are directly assigned to properties of the component; hence property name and parameter name must match. However, parameter names match with property names and are case insensitive.

Currently, Blazor does not support optional parameter. If you want optional parameter, define two routes: one with parameter and another without parameter (refer following code snippet—`RouteParameter.razor`).

```
@page /routingpara
@page /routingpara/{name}
<h3>Route Parameter Example</h3>

<h4>Your name: @Name </h4>

@code {
    [Parameter]
    public string Name { get; set; }

}
```

With preceding code, **Name** property value set to null when the route does not contain the parameter. When the route parameter contains a value, it automatically binds with **Name** property (refer *Figure 3.9: Route Parameter example*):

Figure 3.9: Route Parameter example

You can also define multiple routes for the component, but routes must unique within components.

Route constraints

Route constraints allow you to bind specific types of parameter value to the property. It enforces type matching defined in route with the property data type. It verifies the URL and converts the value to the CLR type using the invariant culture.

Example

Following code enforce, parameter ID must be a type of int. If user pass ID value other than int, the router would not able to find matching route hence return `Notfoundcontent` as a response:

```
@page /routingcons/{id:int}

    <h3>Route Constraints Example</h3>

<h4>Id: @Id </h4>

@code {

    [Parameter]

    public int Id { get; set; }


}
```

Blazor support for following route constraints. As you have seen here, route constraints matching for some of the types are always invariant culture.

Constraint	Invariant culture matching	Example	Example Matches
int	Yes	{id:int}	895, 598, -569, -456987
long	Yes	{id:long}	895, 598, -569, -456987
float	Yes	{price:float}	1.25, 1.5e10, 1,265
double	Yes	{price:double}	1.25, 1.5e10, 1,265
decimal	Yes	{price:decimal}	55.65, 1,502.56
guid	No	{id:guid}	4d019947-e29f-4540-a686-c536c16521b8
bool	No	{enabled:bool}	True, false
datetime	Yes	{joiningdate:datetime}	2019-10-25, 2018-02-14 07:45 pm

Table 3.2: Supported Route constraints

The navigation in the Blazor app can occur in two ways:

- Using `Anchor` tag on page and user click on same to navigate
- Using the `NavLink` tag. It is introduced in Blazor. It automatically sets a working CSS class if the route is matched.

Example:

```
<a href=/test1>Anchor tag</a>

<NavLink href=/test2 Match=NavLinkMatch.All>NavLink</NavLink>
```

The `NavLink` tag has `Match` property (`NavLinkMatch` enum type) that tells Blazor app to the active navigation bar. There is two option for `NavLinkMatch`:

- `NavLinkMatch.All`: if entire URL match then the NavLink is active
- `NavLinkMatch.Prefix`: If any prefix of the URL then the NavLink is active

Blazor app sets a working CSS class when the route is matched according to the match option sets.

Programmatically navigate one component to another component

You can also navigate from one component to another component in C# code using `Microsoft.AspNetCore.Components.IUriHelper`. This helper provides the following events and methods:

Event / Method	Description
NavigateTo	It navigates to specified URI. If the forceload parameter is set to true, client-side routing is bypassed, and the browser is forced to load a new page
GetAbsoluteUri	Gets the current absolute URI
GetBaseUri	Gets the base URI with trailing slash
ToAbsoluteUri	It converts relative URI to absolute URI
ToBaseRelativePath	Returns relative URI with base URI prefix
OnLocationChanged	This event is fired when browser location has changed

Table 3.3: IUriHelper Methods

First, you need to inject the IUriHelper service into components to navigate from one component to another using C# code. You can inject the service dependency using @inject directive or inject attribute to your component.

Following is example, when a user clicks on the button, the page is navigated to new URI (`nextcomponent`):

```
@using Microsoft.AspNetCore.Components;

@page /programmaticallynavigate
@inject IUriHelper UriHelper
```

```
<h3>Programmatically Navigate one component to another component</h3>

<button @onclick=ButtonClicked>Programatically Change Routing</button>

@code {
    void ButtonClicked()
    {
        UriHelper.NavigateTo(nextcomponent);
    }
}
```

You will learn more about injecting the dependency in the next chapter.

Query parameters

The query string or query parameter is the most common method to pass data from one component to another component by defined data in URI. The namespace `Microsoft.AspNetCore.WebUtilities` contains `QueryHelpers` class that helps you to access query string and query parameters within the component. Using the `ParseQuery` method of this class, you can extract the value from the query string.

Following code snippet shows the example of accessing query parameter in component:

```
@using Microsoft.AspNetCore.Components;
@using Microsoft.AspNetCore.WebUtilities;

@page /queryparameter
@inject IUriHelper UriHelper
<h3>Query Parameter Example</h3>

<p>Name : @Name</p>

@code {
    public string Name { get; set; }
    protected override void OnInitialized()
    {
        var uri = new Uri(UriHelper.GetAbsoluteUri());
        Name = QueryHelpers.ParseQuery(uri.Query).TryGetValue(name, out
var type) ? type.First() : ;
```

```
    }
}
```

The `ParseQuery` method returns the dictionary of type `Dictionary<string, StringValues>` that contains all query parameters of the route. As you have seen in *Figure 3.10: Query parameter example,* query parameter or query string value fetch using `ParseQuery` method, and you can bind it to any property:

Figure 3.10: Query parameter example

Blazor provides similar type routing as ASP.NET core provides. There are some features not supported by Blazor but supported in ASP.NET core. In the nearest future, Blazor supports all the features supported in ASP.NET core.

Forms and validation

The data validation is essential for any application. It helps you to protect invalid data injected into your database. Using data annotation, Blazor supports forms and validation. Blazor introduced the `EditForm` component that use to define a form in-app.

Data annotations

The validation is very critical for any application. To do the validation, the developer writes many if-else conditions and makes it more complicated. It might have defective code and take more time to test. The data annotations help you to reduce such complexity by reducing code that is written for validation. It is decorated with attribute to model. It allows to leverage the same annotations for client-side validations in some .NET applications such as MVC.

There are many built-in data annotation attributes available such as `Required`, `StringLength`, `Range`, `EmailAddress`, `Phone`, `RegularExpression`, and so on. You can also create your validation attribute that suits for your business rules.

In the following code snippet, `EmployeeModel` class contains a couple of properties and all properties decorated with data annotation:

```
public class EmployeeModel
{
    [Required]
    [StringLength(50, ErrorMessage = First Name is too long)]
    public string FirstName { get; set; }
    public string LastName { get; set; }
    [Required]
    [StringLength(10, ErrorMessage = Code is too long)]
    public string Code { get; set; }
    [Required]
    [Range(1, 150, ErrorMessage = Invalid Age. It must be between 1 to
150.)]
    public int Age { get; set; }
    [Required]
    public DateTime? DateOfJoining { get; set; }
}
```

You can also define multiple data annotations for a single property.

Edit Forms and validation components

Using the `EditForm` component, you can define the form in the Blazor app. The `DataAnnotationsValidator` component tells the Blazor engine to do the validation using data annotation. You can summarize validation messages using the `ValidationSummary` component. Blazor form is also provided `OnValidSubmit` event that triggered when the form successfully submits and `OnInvalidSubmit` event when the form has validation error on submit. Alternatively, you can also use the `OnSubmit` event to trigger the validation. Following code snippet shows how to validate with Blazor component:

```
<EditForm Model=@employee OnValidSubmit=@HandleValidSubmit>
    <DataAnnotationsValidator />
    <ValidationSummary />
...
...
</EditForm>
```

There are many built-in input components available that receive and validate user inputs. This component is made in such a way that when they are changed, and form is submitted, validation is fired. The following are available input components.

Component	Render as
InputText	`<input>`
InputCheckbox	`<input type=checkbox>`
InputNumber	`<input type=number>`
InputTextArea	`<textarea>`
InputSelect	`<select>`
InputDate	`<input type=date>`

Table 3.4: Built-in input components

These components are also providing default behavior such as validating data on edit and changing CSS class. Also, some input control, such as `InputNumber` and `InputDate`, includes parsing logic.

In following example, form validates user input based on data annotation defined in `EmployeeModel`:

```
@page /
@using FormsAndValidation.Data;
<h3>Validation Example</h3>
<br />
<hr />
<EditForm Model=@employee OnValidSubmit=@HandleValidSubmit>
    <DataAnnotationsValidator />
    <div class=row content>
        <div class=col-md-2><label for=firstname>First Name</label></div>
        <div class=col-md-3><InputText id=firstname @bind-Value=@employ-
ee.FirstName /></div>
    </div>
    <div class=row content>
        <div class=col-md-2><label for=lastname>Last Name</label></div>
        <div class=col-md-3><InputText id=lastname @bind-Value=@employ-
ee.LastName /></div>
    </div>
    <div class=row content>
```

```
        <div class=col-md-2><label for=code>Code</label></div>

        <div class=col-md-3><InputText id=code @bind-Value=@employee.
Code /></div>

    </div>

    <div class=row content>

        <div class=col-md-2><label for=age>Age</label></div>

        <div class=col-md-1><InputNumber id=age @bind-Value=@employee.
Age /></div>

    </div>

    <div class=row content>

        <div class=col-md-2><label for=dateofjoining>Date Of Joining</
label></div>

        <div class=col-md-1><InputDate id=dateofjoining @bind-Value=@
employee.DateOfJoining /></div>

    </div>

    <div class=row content>

        <button type=submit>Submit</button>

    </div>

    <br />

    <div class=row>

        <ValidationSummary />

    </div>


</EditForm>


@code {

    private EmployeeModel employee = new EmployeeModel();


    private void HandleValidSubmit()

    {

        Console.WriteLine(OnValidSubmit);

    }

}
```

As you have seen in following *Figure 3.11: Validation Example: validation summary,* the invalid data CSS is applied and validation message list down in summary when input having invalid data:

Figure 3.11: Validation Example: validation summary

The `ValidationSummary` component shows summarize validation messages. You can also display validation messages for specific input control. It can be achieved using the `ValidationMessage` component. With this component, you must specify the model property name using for attribute.

```
<ValidationMessage For=@(() => @employee.FirstName) />
```

As you have seen in the following *Figure 3.12: Validation Example: ValidationMessage,* the invalid data CSS is applied, and an individual validation message is shown when input having invalid data:

Figure 3.12: Validation Example: ValidationMessage

Blazor provides rich support for validation. It automatically applied or remove invalid CSS (red color border) based on input change.

Summary

- **Blazor support one-way and two-way databinding:**
  - o One-way binding:
    - • One-way binding allows you to bind value variables/properties to the HTML element in DOM.
    - • Add @ prefix to variable/property name to achieve One-way databinding.
  - o Two-way binding:
    - • The two-way binding allows you to bind the value of variables/properties to the HTML element in DOM and vice-versa.
    - • It is achieved by the `@bind` attribute.
    - • The changes are not reflected immediately with the `@bind` attribute as it registers the onchange event.
    - • The `@bind-value` attribute allows you to bind an event that fires when the value gets changed.
    - • The `@bind` attribute also supports for culture parameter (`@bind:culture`) that parsing and formatting a value before binding to HTML element to assigned culture.
    - • Using `@bind:format` attribute, you can format the date.

- **Event binding:**
  - o You can register the event of any HTML element using the `@on{event}` attribute. Here, the event is the name of the event.
  - o The event arguments are also allowed for some events. It is not mandatory to define the event argument in the method definition.

- **Layout:**
  - o The layout page helps you to do a consistent look and feel throughout the application and prevent to write duplicate code.
  - o You can specify a layout for the component using the `@layout` directive and Layout attribute.
  - o The different components may have different layout pages.
  - o The layout page defined in `_Imports.razor` file applied to all Razor pages in the folder hierarchy.
  - o Blazor supports the nested layouts.

- **Routing:**
  - o Routing is a process of a match URL pattern.
  - o The default route for the Blazor server application is defined in `_Host.razor (@page /)`.
  - o Routing can be done using the `@page` directive or `RouteAttribute`.
  - o You can also define multiple routes for a single component.
  - o Using the route parameter, you can pass to any component when it initializes.
  - o Blazor does not support the optional route parameter.
  - o Route constraints allow you to bind specific types of parameters to property value.

- **Forms and validations:**
  - o You can define a form using the EditForm component.
  - o The `DataAnnotationsValidator` component tells the Blazor engine to do the validation using data annotation.
  - o There are two options to display error messages on the screen.
  - o **Summarized error messages:** this can be achieved using the `ValidationSummary` component.
  - o **Individual error message:** this can be achieved using the ValidationMessage component. With this component, you must specify the model property name using for attribute for all fields that you want to perform validation.
  - o There are built-in input components available to receive and validate input. These components automatically change the CSS classes to reflect field state.
  - o Some input control, such as `InputNumber` and `InputDate`, includes parsing logic.

What you learned in this chapter?

In this chapter, you will learn about Blazor core concepts such as data and event binding, the concept of layout page, routing, route parameter, route constraints, query parameter, form, and validation. Also, learn about the essential directives and attributes used to describe the core concept.

What is next?

Dependency injection is a design pattern that helps you to create a loosely coupled application. It provides excellent maintainability, testability, and re-usability. Blazor has built-in support for dependency injection. In the next chapter, you will learn about the dependency injection and how to inject service into the component.

Questions

1. Explain data and event binding in the Blazor app?
2. What is EventCallBack?
3. How can you format the date with two-way binding?
4. What is the use of the StateHasChanged method?
5. What are events supported to UIEventArgs?
6. What is the use of the layout page?
7. How to define layout page globally?
8. What is routing?
9. How to set a route parameter with the Blazor app?
10. Does Blazor support an optional parameter?
11. What is the use of route constraints?
12. How can you validate the Blazor app?
13. What is the use of the ValidationSummary and ValidationMessage component?

CHAPTER 4

Dependency Injection

Introduction

Dependency injection is a design pattern that helps you to create a loosely coupled application. It provides excellent maintainability, testability, and re-usability.

In this chapter, we'll cover the following topics

- Types of dependency injection
- Service lifetime
- Add services to the application
- Default services
- Inject the service in the component
- Use dependency in services
- Using OwningComponentBase

Objective

- Understand Dependency injection and how to inject
- Understand how to inject dependency in Blazor App
- Understand default service in Blazor App
- Understand OwningComponentBase class and its usage

Types of dependency injection

With DI, dependency required to complete is injected from the outer world rather than created them inside the functions/methods of the class.

You can inject the dependency by one of the following three ways:

Construction injection

In this type, class dependencies are injected at the constructor level. It means that when you create the instance of the class, the class dependencies must inject. It provides a strong dependency contract between objects.

Setter injection

It is also known as property injection. Here, class dependencies are provided using properties instead of the constructor. It provides loose dependency binding between objects. It allows you to pass dependencies when they required instead of the pass at the time of creating instance.

Interface based injection

It can be achieved by using a familiar interface, and all classes are implements this interface to inject the dependency. It is used with a combination of either constructor injection or setter injection.

ASP.NET Core provides built-in support for dependency injection. It is not limited to middleware but also supports in model, view, controller, and Razor pages. There are many built-in services available with ASP.NET core. Formally, built-in services are known as framework services. You can also create custom services formally known as application services.

Blazor also supports the same type of **dependency injection (DI)** that provided by ASP.NET core. You can inject built-in services into the Blazor component to use them. You can also inject custom service by define and register them in the app.

Service lifetime

You can also specify the lifetime for registered services. The service instance gets disposed of when the specified lifetime reached. The service life can be configured using the following three type:

Scoped

Using the scoped method, the service instance created and shared per request to the application. The single service instance available for request. The service instance created in every request.

The **Blazor WebAssembly (Client)** does not support the concept of dependency injection scopes. They behave like singleton service. Blazor server app supports this concept, but the scope is limited to the connection. So, it is useful when services should be scoped to the current user.

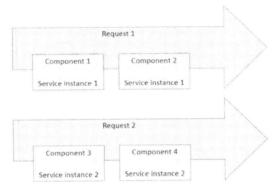

Figure 4.1: Scoped service lifetime

As shown in the preceding figure, there is a single service instance per request with a Scoped service lifetime.

Singleton

It creates and shares the single instance of service in application life. It is more like a singleton design pattern, but you do not care about the implementation, it maintained by the Blazor app.

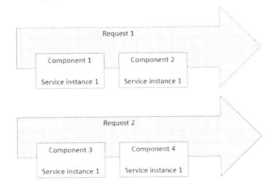

Figure 4.2: Singleton service lifetime

As shown in the preceding figure, there is a single service instance shared in the entire application with a singleton service lifetime.

Transient

It creates the instance of service whenever you ask for it. Service should be very lightweight when you add service in this way. Blazor app always creates a new service instance when it is injected into the component. It means that every component has its instance of service if service injected in the component.

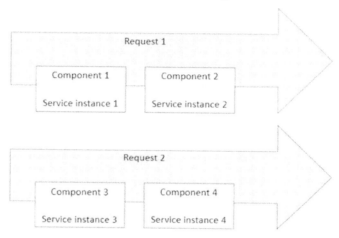

Figure 4.3: Transient service lifetime

As shown in the preceding figure, every component has its instance of service with transient service lifetime.

Add services to the application

You can add services (framework or application) to an app in the `ConfigureService` method of startup class. It takes `IServiceCollection` as a parameter that is a list of service descriptor objects. Service can be added to service descriptor objects based on the service life you required. Use the `AddSingleton` method to add service as a singleton lifetime, use the `AddTransient` method to add service as transient lifetime, and use the `AddScoped` method to add service as a scoped lifetime.

Following is a code snippet to add service as Scoped lifetime:

```
public void ConfigureServices(IServiceCollection services)
{
    ...
```

```
    ...
    services.AddScoped<IMyService, MyService>();
    ...
}
```

Following is a code snippet to add service as Transient lifetime:

```
public void ConfigureServices(IServiceCollection services)
{
    ...
    ...
    services.AddTransient<IMyService, MyService>();
    ...
}
```

Following is a code snippet to add service as Singleton lifetime:

```
public void ConfigureServices(IServiceCollection services)
{
    ...
    ...
    services. AddSingleton<IMyService, MyService>();
    ...
}
```

The method described previously is a prevalent method to add services. You can also add services using the following methods:

Methods	Disposed object automatically	Multiple	Pass args?
Add{LIFETIME}<{SERVICE}, {IMPLE-MENTATION}>() Example: services.AddScoped<IMySer, My-Ser>();	Yes	Yes	No

`Add{LIFETIME}<{SERVICE}>(sp => new {IMPLEMENTATION})`
 	
Example:
 	
`services.AddScoped< IMySer >(sp => new MySer ());`
	Yes	Yes	Yes

`Add{LIFETIME}<{SERVICE}>(sp => new {IMPLEMENTATION})`
 	
Example:
 	
`services.AddScoped< IMySer >(sp => new MySer ());`
	Yes	Yes	Yes

`Add{LIFETIME}<{SERVICE}>(new {IM-PLEMENTATION})`
 	
Example:
 	
`services.AddScoped<IMySer>(new My-Ser ());`
	No	Yes	Yes

`Add{LIFETIME}(new {IMPLEMENTA-TION})`
 	
Example:
 	
`services.AddScoped(new MySer());`
	No	No	Yes

Table 4.1: Common methods to add service

You can also use `TryAdd{LIFETIME}` methods that only register the service if an implementation already registered. This method is under `Microsoft.Extensions.DependencyInjection.Extensions` namespace. You can use either `TryAdd`, `TryAddTransient`, `TryAddScoped`, or `TryAddSingleton` method to register the service.

`services.TryAddSingleton<IMyService>(MyService);`

Apart from this, `TryAddEnumerable(ServiceDescriptor)` methods are also available that register the service if the same type of service is not already registered. It used to register multiple services having the same implementation. In the following example, `Class MyService` implements both `IMyService1` and `IMyService2` interface:

`public interface IMyService1 { }`

```
public interface IMyService2 { }

public class MyService : IMyService1, IMyService2 { }
```

First line of following code is registered implementation of IMyService1 and second line registered implementation of IMyService2:

```
services.TryAddEnumerable(ServiceDescriptor.Singleton<IMyService1, My-
Service>());

services.TryAddEnumerable(ServiceDescriptor.Singleton<IMyService2, My-
Service>());
```

If you are trying to re-register the service, this method ignores the registration statement as service is already registered.

Default services

There are few default services in Blazor application those are automatically added to the service collection. These services are added with a specific life, and you do not need to add them. The following are the services added by default.

Service	Lifetime	Description
HttpClient	Singleton	It provides the method for sending and receiving HTTP request/response. This service sets the base address of URI automatically using HttpClient.BaseAddress
IJSRuntime	Singleton	This service provides API related to JavaScript interop. It is an instance of JavaScript runtime for JavaScript calls
NavigationManager	Singleton	It contains the API for working with URIs and navigation state

Table 4.2: Default services

Note that custom service providers are not provided default services automatically to use in service. If you want to use default services with a custom service provider, you need to add these services to a new service provider.

Inject the service in the component

Once you have added services in service collection, they are available to use within the component. You can inject the service to the Razor component by using the @inject directive. It contains two parameters: **service type and service instance name**. The service instance name is just like property that you can access within the component, but you don't care about creating a property, the compiler will take care.

You can also use multiple `@inject` directives for injecting different services to the Blazor component.

Syntax:

`@inject ServiceType InstanceName`

Example:

`@inject IMyService MyService`

You can inject the service to class-based / code behind of component using Inject attribute. The `@inject` directive is converted to this attribute when the Blazor app compiled and generate a class file for the component. This attribute can only be used with the class-based component.

```
public class ClassOnly : ComponentBase
{
    [Inject]
    protected IEmployeeService EmployeeService { get; set; }
...
...
}
```

Example of adding service as a dependency

The following example shows simple steps to create and add the service to service collection using DI. The service is created as the first step. Here, the service class is implemented using the interface. It is not necessary for service class to implement the interface. It is an excellent design pattern that you implement the interface to create service. The service contains the `GetEmployees` method that returns all available employees; however, demo returns hardcoded employee list.

EmployeeService.cs:

```
namespace DIExample.Data
{
    using DIExample.Model;
    using System.Threading.Tasks;
    public interface IEmployeeService
    {
        Task<Employee[]> GetEmployees();
    }
```

```
public class EmployeeService : IEmployeeService
{
    public Task<Employee[]> GetEmployees()
    {
        var employees = new Employee[2];
        employees[0] = new Employee { Id = 1, Code = "EMP01",
                    FirstName = "Jignesh", LastName = "Trivedi" };
        employees[1] = new Employee { Id = 2, Code = "EMP02",
                    FirstName = "Tejas", LastName = "Trivedi" };
        return Task.FromResult(employees);
    }
}
}
```

The next step is to add service to service container in ConfigureServices method of Startup class. As you aware, there are three options available for different lifetime of service. Base on your need, you can use any one of them.

Startup.cs:

```
public void ConfigureServices(IServiceCollection services)
{
    ...
    ...
    services.AddSingleton<IEmployeeService, EmployeeService>();
    ...
}
```

If you do not register the service to the service container, the component is not able to find service from the service container; hence throw an exception as following (refer *Figure 4.4: Exception If service not registered*).

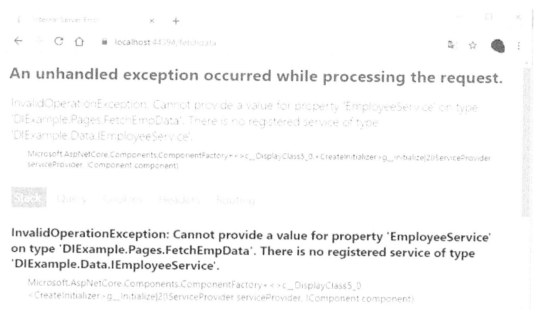

Figure 4.4: Exception If service not registered

Now service is available to use in the Blazor component. Using @inject directive, you can inject the service. If your component having a code-behind class file or you have class only component, then you can inject service using inject attribute.

FetchEmpData.razor:

```
@page "/fetchdata"

@using DIExample.Data
@inject IEmployeeService EmployeeService

<h3>Employee List</h3>
...
...
...

@code {
    Employee[] employees;
```

```
protected override async Task OnInitializedAsync()
{
    employees = await EmployeeService.GetEmployees();
}
}
```

Following is the output when the above code has been run:

Figure 4.5: output - Employee list

Here, all employee list is populated (refer *Figure 4.5: output - Employee list)* however example shows hardcode value, but it may come from the database.

Use dependency in services

Your service might have complex scenarios such as your service make a further call to another service over HTTP using default service `HttpClient`. The default services are not to be added using `@inject` directive or Inject attribute. You must have to use constructor injection. The default service is added to the service's constructor. In this scenario, you must register your service using the `AddHttpClient` method instead of `AddTransient`, `AddSingleton`, and `AddScoped` in `ConfigureService` method of `Startup` class.

Following code shows service definition and inject default service (`HttpClient`):

```
public class EmployeeServiceNew : IEmployeeService
{
    public EmployeeServiceNew(HttpClient client)
```

```
    {
        ...
    }
    ...
    ...
}
```

Following code shows how to add service in request pipeline (Startup.cs):

```
public void ConfigureServices(IServiceCollection services)
{
    ...

    ...

    services.AddHttpClient<IEmployeeService, EmployeeServiceNew>();

    ...
}
```

Using OwningComponentBase

You learned about Scoped service in the preceding section. Once the request has been completed, scoped or transient must be disposed by the DI system. With Blazor server application, scope duration up to the connection that results in scoped service available much longer time than expected and behaves like singleton service. To limit the service life to scoped to the component, you can use `OwningComponentBase` or `OwningComponentBase<T> base class`.

All the Blazor components inherit from ComponentBase class, and `OwningComponentBase` class is also inherited from `ComponentBase` class. So, you can also inherit the Blazor component from `OwningComponentBase` instead of `ComponentBase` class. These base classes provide single service that can be accessed using property `Service`:

```
@page "/fetchdata1"

@using DIExample.Data

@inherits OwningComponentBase<IEmployeeService>

<h3>Employee List</h3>

...
```

```
. . .
. . .
@code {
    Employee[] employees;

    protected override async Task OnInitializedAsync()
    {
        employees = await Service.GetEmployees();
    }
}
```

This base class gets the required service from `IServiceCollection` and set `Service` property. You can only access a single service using this method of injecting service; however, it provides scope to the lifetime of the component. The instance of service is disposed of when the component is disposed of.

Summary

- Dependency Injection is a design pattern that helps you to create a loosely coupled application
- ASP.NET Core provides built-in support for dependency injection
- You can inject the dependency using
  o Construction injection
    - Class dependencies are injected at constructor level
    - It provides firm dependency contract between objects
  o Setter injection
    - It is also known as property injection
    - Class dependencies are provided using properties
    - It provides loose dependency binding between objects
  o Interface based injection
    - The familiar interface used to implement class and this interface used to inject the dependency
    - It is used with a combination of either constructor injection or setter injection
- You can also specify the lifetime for registered services
  o Scoped:
    - Service instance available for request only

- • The service instance created in every request
- • Blazor client does not support this concept, and in Blazor server, the scope is limited to connection
  - o Singleton:
    - • It creates and shares the single instance of service in the application of life
  - o Transient:
    - • It creates the instance of service whenever requested
    - • Blazor app always create new service instance when it injected to component
- • You can add services (framework or application) to an app in `ConfigureService` method of the startup class
- • You can also use `TryAdd{LIFETIME}` methods that only register the service if an implementation already registered
- • Blazor application provides three default services that automatically added to the service collection
- • The `@inject` directive and Inject attribute can be used to add service dependency in component
- • There are three easy steps to use dependency injection into Blazor application
  - o Create the service
  - o Register the service
  - o Inject the service in the component
- • The `OwningComponentBase` class can help you to control the lifetime of service to scope for a component

What you learned in this chapter?

In this chapter, you have learned about dependency injection and different types of dependency injection, service lifetime, and different types of service lifetime supported by Blazor App, default services, and usage of `OwningComponentBase` class.

What next?

As you know, communication between UI and server code is done using SignalR, and it uses JavaScript interop to do this. In this next chapter, you will learn about the JavaScript interop. Using JavaScript interop, you can call JavaScript function from C# code and vice versa.

Questions

1. What is Dependency injection, and what are the different ways to inject your dependency?

2. What is service lifetime for dependency and explain different lifetime supported by ASP.NET Core?

3. What is the default service in the Blazor app?

4. Using which directive or attribute, you can add a dependency in the Blazor component?

5. Explain the usage of OwningComponentBase class in the Blazor App?

CHAPTER 5

JavaScript Interop

Introduction

Blazor applications use the JavaScript library to bootstrap; typically, it is `blazor.server.js,` and Blazor also supports any JavaScript library. With Blazor, you can call **JavaScript function** from C# (.NET) code and vice versa. This feature refers to JavaScript Interop. As you know, the Blazor server app uses SignalR to do communication between UI and server code. The SignalR uses JavaScript Interop to call browser API and DOM manipulation.

In this chapter, we'll cover the following topics

- What is JavaScript Interop?
- Invoke JavaScript functions from .NET methods
- Invoke .NET (C#) function from JavaScript
- Capture references to elements
- Detect when a Blazor app is pre-rendering
- Share interop code in a class library

Objective

- Understand JavaScript Interop
- Understand how to invoke JavaScript function from C# code and vice versa
- Understand how to invoke JavaScript Interop when Blazor app is pre-rendering
- Understand how to access HTML elements from C# code
- Understand how to invoke interop from the shared class library

What is JavaScript Interop?

Blazor client is running on WebAssembly, and the Blazor server does not require WebAssembly to run the application. There are lot of things which could not be possible without using JavaScript for Blazor Server and WebAssembly applications, for example, DOM manipulation and accessing browser API. The JavaScript Interop can help you to resolve these problems. Using JavaScript Interop, you can call JavaScript function from your C# (.NET) code and vice versa.

Invoke JavaScript functions from C# (.NET) methods

There are many scenarios where you need to call JavaScript function from your C#(.NET) code as JavaScript can call API to expose browser capabilities. Using `IJSRuntime` abstraction, you can call JavaScript function from your C# (.NET) code. The `InvokeAsync<T>` method of `IJSRuntime` abstraction is used to invoked JavaScript function. This function takes two parameters: identifier and arguments. The identifier is the name of a JavaScript function that you want to invoke, and arguments are the function parameters that any number of JSON serializable objects. The identifier is defined as the global scope by default; however, you can define the scope of the identifier. The JavaScript function must return type `T`, and JSON serializable. Following code shows the signatures of `InvokeAsync` methods define in `IJSRuntime` abstraction and its extensions:

```
ValueTask<TValue> InvokeAsync<TValue>(string identifier, object[] args);

ValueTask<TValue> InvokeAsync<TValue>(string identifier, CancellationToken cancellationToken, params object[] args);

ValueTask<TValue> InvokeAsync<TValue>( string identifier, TimeSpan timeout, params object[] args);
```

The `JSRuntimeExtensions` class also contain `InvokeVoidAsync` method that call JavaScript function return `void(0)` or `void 0` or undefined. Following code shows the signatures of `InvokeVoidAsync` methods defined in `IJSRuntime` extension:

```
ValueTask InvokeVoidAsync(this IJSRuntime jsRuntime, string identifier,
params object[] args);

ValueTask InvokeVoidAsync(this IJSRuntime jsRuntime, string identifier,
CancellationToken cancellationToken, params object[] args);

ValueTask InvokeVoidAsync(this IJSRuntime jsRuntime, string identifier,
TimeSpan timeout, params object[] args);
```

You can also call the JavaScript function defined in the file (.js), and this file must refer to the `Script` tag inside the `<head>` element of either `wwwroot/index.html` (for Blazor Client app) or `Pages/_Host.cshtml` (for Blazor Server app).

There are three steps to call JavaScript function from C# code:
- Create JavaScript function that you want to inject from C# code
- Inject `IJSRuntime` service to the component. It is a default service, so it is not required to add this service in the request pipeline
- Invoke JavaScript function using `InvokeVoidAsync` or `InvokeAsync<T>` method

The `InvokeVoidAsync` and `InvokeAsync` method invoke JavaScript function asynchronously so that you can use await with both methods.

The following example demonstrates how to invoke void JavaScript function from the C# code using the `InvokeVoidAsync` method.

Here, the JavaScript function is straightforward. It does not accept any parameter and not returning any value but shows an alert. Following code snippet shows JavaScript function:

```
function calledJSFunction() {
    alert("JavaScript function called from C# Code!!!");
}
```

As discussed, earlier chapter, if you want to use any service in a component, then first you need to inject it in component using `@inject` directive or `inject` attribute in code behind then it must inject in a component. To use JavaScript Interop, you need to `IJSRuntime` service into the component.

In this example, the C# function `CallVoidJSFunction` is called on button click, and inside the function, it calls JavaScript function using `IJSRuntime` service. Following code snippet shows the component code:

```
@page "/example"
@inject IJSRuntime JsRuntime;

<h3>JavaScript Interop Example</h3>

<h4> Example 1: Call void JS Function</h4>
<br />
<button class="btn btn-primary" @onclick="CallVoidJSFunction">Call Void
JS Function</button>

@code {
    private void CallVoidJSFunction()
    {
        JsRuntime.InvokeVoidAsync("calledJSFunction", null);
    }
}
```

When you run preceding code and click on the button, a JavaScript function is invoked and shows alert (refer *Figure 5.1: JavaScript void function call from C# code):*

Figure 5.1: JavaScript void function call from C# code

The following example demonstrates how to invoke the JavaScript function that accepts the argument and returns some value from the C# code using the **InvokeAsync** method.

Here, the JavaScript function is straightforward. It accepts integer **array** and returns the **sum** of array elements:

```
function addNumbers(numbers) {
    if (!Array.isArray(numbers)) {
```

```
        return 0;
    }
    var sum = 0;
    for (var i = 0; i < numbers.length; i++) {
        sum = sum + numbers[i];
    }
    return sum;
}
```

In this example, the C# function **AddNumbers** is called on button click and inside the function it calls JavaScript function using **IJSRuntime** service and pass the integer array. Following code snippet shows the component code:

```
@page "/example"
@inject IJSRuntime JsRuntime;


<h3>JavaScript Interop Example</h3>


<h4> Example 2: Call JS Function with parameter and return value</h4>
<br />
<button class="btn btn-primary" @onclick="AddNumbers">Add numbers</but-
ton>
<p>Total sum of array: @sum</p>
<hr>
@code {

    private int[] array = new int[5] { 2, 3, 56, 76, 45 };
    private int sum = 0;


    private async Task AddNumbers()
    {
        sum = await JsRuntime.InvokeAsync<int>("addNumbers", array);
    }
}
```

When you run preceding code and click on the button, a JavaScript function is invoked, and this function returns the sum of array elements (refer *Figure 5.2: JavaScript function with parameter and return value call from C# code*):

Figure 5.2: JavaScript function with parameter and return value call from C# code

With the Blazor server app, the calling of JavaScript function in the pre-rendering event is not possible as the connection between server and browser has not yet been established. You will learn more about this in the upcoming section of this chapter.

Invoke C# (.NET) methods from JavaScript

It is also possible to call a C# (.NET) method from the JavaScript in Blazor app. Blazor provides two methods: `DotNet.invokeMethod` and DotNet.invokeMethodAsync to call C# (.NET) method from the JavaScript. Here, you need to pass three arguments: assembly name that contains the function, function name, and function arguments, if any. It is recommended to use `DotNet.invokeMethodAsync` method with the Blazor server app. To call the C# method from JavaScript, it must have the following characteristics:

- C# method must be define as public
- C# method must be decorate with JSInvokable attribute
- Method name (or its identifier) must be unique across the assembly
- Currently, generic methods are not supported
- The method can be defined as static or instance

Optionally, you can pass an identifier name with the `JSInvokable` attribute. The method name becomes an identifier by default if you do not pass the identifier with the `JSInvokable` attribute.

In following example, JavaScript called C# (.NET) function by calling `DotNet.invokeMethodAsync`. Here, you have to pass the identifier name and assembly namespace with this method:

```
function CallCSFunction() {
    DotNet.invokeMethodAsync("JavaScriptInterop", "CalledByJavaScript")
    .then(data => {
        alert(data);
    });
}
```

In the preceding code JavaScript method is being called on click of HTML button. The C# code section contains `CalledByJavaScript` method and this method decorated with `JSInvokable` attribute:

```
@page "/example2"
@inject IJSRuntime JsRuntime;
<h3>JavaScript Interop Example</h3>

<h4> Example 1: Call void C# Function</h4>


<button class="btn btn-primary" onclick="CallCSFunction()">Call Void C# Function</button>


@code  {
    [JSInvokable]
    public static string CalledByJavaScript()
    {
        return "Hello Reader!!!";
    }
}
```

When you run preceding code and click on the button, it calls CS method and returns string message, and it shows by JavaScript alert (refer *Figure 5.3: C# method (without parameter) called from JavaScript)*:

Figure 5.3: C# method (without parameter) called from JavaScript

In another example, integer array is passed to the C# method from the JavaScript function. It returns the sum of all array elements. Following code snippet shows the JavaScript function definition:

```
function csAddNumbers() {
    var array = [2, 3, 4, 56, 78];
    DotNet.invokeMethodAsync("JavaScriptInterop", "AddNumbers", array)
        .then(data => {
            document.getElementById('lblSum').innerText = data;
        });
}
```

Same as previous example, the JavaScript function called by clicking on HTML button. The C# method returns the sum of all array element and JavaScript function shows it in a label (refer following code):

```
@page "/example2"
@inject IJSRuntime JsRuntime;
<h3>JavaScript Interop Example</h3>


<h4> Example 2: Call C# Function with parameter and return value</h4>


<button class="btn btn-primary" onclick="csAddNumbers()">Add numbers</button>
```

```
<p>Total sum:<label id="lblSum">0</label></p>

<hr>


@code  {


    [JSInvokable]

    public static int AddNumbers(int[] data)

    {

        return data.Sum();

    }

}
```

When you run preceding code and click on the button, it calls CS method and returns string message, and it shows by JavaScript alert (refer *Figure 5.4: C# method with parameter and return type called from JavaScript*):

Figure 5.4: *C# method with parameter and return type called from JavaScript*

In the preceding example, C# static methods are being called from the JavaScript function, but it is also possible to call the instance method from a JavaScript function. Following code, snippet shows the class that contains the `AddNumberInstance` non-static method:

```
public class InstanceMethodHelper

{

    [JSInvokable]

    public int AddNumberInstance(int[] data)

    {

        return data.Sum();
```

```
    }
}
```

To invoke the C# instance method from JavaScript function, you need to pass .NET instance to JavaScript using the `Create method of DotNetObjectReference` class.

It is not necessary to pass .NET class instance when JavaScript or Blazor component is loading. You can pass .NET class instance to JavaScript any point of time, for example, button click. In the following example, the .NET class instance is created and passed to the JavaScript on the `OnInitializedAsync` method of the component life cycle. Here, `IJSRuntime.InvokeAsync` method has been used to pass the instance of C# class:

```
@page "/example2"

@inject IJSRuntime JsRuntime;

<h3>JavaScript Interop Example</h3>

<h4> Example 3: Call C# instance method</h4>

<button class="btn btn-primary" onclick="csInstanceAddNumbers()">Add
numbers (instance)</button>

<p>Total sum:<label id="lblSumIns">0</label></p>

@code {

    protected override async Task OnInitializedAsync()
    {
        await JsRuntime.InvokeAsync<object>("passInstanceToJS", DotNeto-
bjectReference.Create(new InstanceMethodHelper()));
    }


    ...
    ...
}
```

In preceding code snippet, `passInstanceToJS` JavaScript method called from C# and it stores the C# class instance to any JavaScript variable (refer following code):

```
var myClsObj;

function passInstanceToJS(instance) {
```

```
    myClsObj = instance;
}
```

Now, you can invoke C# instance method on passed instance using `invokeMethod` or `invokeMethodAsync` functions:

```
function csInstanceAddNumbers() {
    var array = [12, 31, 4, 56, 78];
    return myClsObj.invokeMethodAsync('AddNumberInstance', array)
        .then(data => {
            document.getElementById('lblSumIns').innerText = data;
        });
}
```

You can call the C# instance method from the JavaScript function by preceding code in the Blazor app. It is standard for both the Blazor client app and the Blazor server app.

Capture references to elements

In some scenarios, you require an HTML element reference. With the Blazor app, you can capture a reference to the HTML element in a component. It can be achieved using the `@ref` directive and define the `ElementReference` type in the code section. The `@ref` directive used in HTML to capture element or component reference and `ElementReference` type variable defined for the same element or component.

In following code snippet, input element reference captured to name variable:

```
<input @ref="name" type="text" />

...

@code {
    ElementReference name;

...

...

}
```

The most common example to use element reference in Blazor app is to set focus (on any event) to HTML element using JavaScript Interop. In following example, input element reference is passed to the JavaScript function (using JavaScript Interop) and JavaScript set focus on element using sent reference:

```
@page "/example3"
@inject IJSRuntime JsRuntime;
<h3>Element Reference</h3>

<input @ref="name" type="text" />
<button class="btn btn-primary" @onclick="SetFocus">Set Focus</button>

@code {
    ElementReference name;
    private void SetFocus()
    {
        JsRuntime.InvokeVoidAsync("setFocusOnName", name);
    }
}
```

The following JavaScript function accept element reference as an argument and set focus:

```
function setFocusOnName(element) {
    element.focus();
}
```

The element reference only available after the component is rendered, so it is better to use element reference in OnAfterRenderAsync or OnAfterRender component life cycle methods or any other element event. The element reference value is null before the OnAfterRender event of component life cycle method.

Detect when a Blazor app is pre-rendering

As you aware, Blazor server app uses SignalR to communicate between UI and server. The server will maintain a connection with the client browser. A specific action (for example, calling into JavaScript) is not available when the Blazor server app is pre-rendering as connection with the browser has not been established.

In such cases, you can use the OnAfterRenderAsync method of the component life cycle as when this event is called, the Blazor app is fully rendered, and the server is connected with the client browser.

Blazor server app always relies on the server. The JavaScript Interop may not work due to some server connection issues, and it treated as unreliable. The Blazor server app wait for a minute to get server connection before JavaScript Interop is being called. You can also modify this time-out value for the entire application or a single JavaScript call.

You can specify time-out value by setting up a configuration value of Blazor middleware (injected using the `AddServerSideBlazor` method in `Configure Services` method of `Startup` class). It will be applied to all the component JavaScript Interop calls:

```
services.AddServerSideBlazor(
    options => options.JSInteropDefaultCallTimeout = TimeSpan.FromSec-
onds(60)
);
```

Optionally, you can also set time-out value for a single call as `InvokeAsync` (or `InvokeVoidAsync`) method argument.

```
var result = await JsRuntime.InvokeAsync<string>("TestJSFunction", Time-
Span.FromSeconds(60), "My name");
```

You can increase or decrease the time-out value based on your requirements.

Share interop code in a class library

You can also include JavaScript Interop code into a class library that allows sharing code between projects, and you can also create NuGet packages. ASP.NET core allows you to create **Razor Class Library (RCL)** project that may contain razor pages, views, controller, and so on. It provides ways to share a common UI component across multiple projects.

The RCL can handle embedding JavaScript resources of assembly and JavaScript files placed under the wwwroot folder. The embedding of the resources is taken care of when RCL builds. The built-in library and NuGet package's JavaScript call handle in a similar fashion.

Summary

- Using JavaScript Interop, you can call JavaScript function from C# (.NET) code and vice versa
- Use `InvokeAsync` or `InvokeVoidAsync` method of `IJSRuntime` to call `JavaScript` function from C# code
- Use `DotNet.invokeMethod` and `DotNet.invokeMethodAsync` method to call C# method from JavaScript code
- To call the C# method from JavaScript, C# method must have the following characteristics:

  o Must define as public

  o Must decorate with `JSInvokable` attribute

  o Method name (or its identifier) must unique across the assembly

  o Method not defined as a generic method

  o The method can be defined as static or instance

- To call the C# instance method from JavaScript, a class instance must pass to JavaScript before invokes a JavaScript function

- You can pass a reference of C# class instance to JavaScript using `Create` method of `DotNetObjectReference` class

- By define `@ref` directive and `ElementReference` type in the code section, you can capture element reference

- You can also share JavaScript Interop code by creating RCL

What you learned in this chapter?

In this chapter, you learned about the JavaScript Interop, how to call C# (.NET) function from JavaScript and vice versa in the Blazor app, and how to capture element reference.

What next?

The Blazor is a stateful application framework. With the Blazor server app, the user state is held in server memory in the circuit. When the Blazor server app is temporarily disconnected from the server due to any reason, the app is trying to reconnect to the original circuit from the server memory. In the next chapter, you will learn about state management and how to persist state for the Blazor server app and Blazor client app.

Questions

1. What is JavaScript Interop?

2. How can you invoke JavaScript function from C# code?

3. How can you invoke the C# method from the JavaScript function?

4. Can the C# instance method be called using JavaScript Interop? If yes, then how?

5. How to capture element reference in then Blazor app?

6. Can JavaScript Interop code be shared in RCL (Razor class Library)?

CHAPTER 6
State Management

Introduction

The Blazor is a stateful application framework. Blazor server app always maintains the connection to the server, and for the Blazor client (WebAssembly) app, there is no need to connect with the server to maintain the state. The Blazor server app maintains state in the circuit on server memory. The state management is essential as it retrieves the original app state from server memory when the app is disconnected from the server for any reason.

You can maintain the user session or circuit using the following ways:

- The value stored in the variable or property of the component instance
- Data stored in service instance (injected using DI)
- Rendered UI (most recent render output)

Blazor server app relies on server memory to store user circuits. Still, the Blazor client app (WebAssembly) can take the advantages of any client-side storage mechanism or can use third party packages.

In this chapter, we'll cover the following topics

- Understand Blazor circuits
- Preserve state across circuits

- Where to persist state
- Third-party browser storage solutions

Objective

- Understand how to maintain user state in Blazor server app
- What are the Third-party browser storage solutions to persist state

Understand Blazor circuits

When the Blazor server app is temporarily disconnected from the server due to any reason like network connection loss, the app tries to reconnect to the original circuit from the server memory. However, an app connecting back to the original state on the server is not always possible due to one of the following reasons:

- The server has release disconnected circuits due to timeout or GC called due to low memory

- In web garden deployment environments where multiple servers and load-balanced available, any server not available at any given time. When a user attempts to connect, the original server not available

- The issue with user browser, a user, might close and reopen the browser, browser close due to exception

The user receives a new circuit (empty state) when a user cannot connect with the original circuit due to any of the above reasons. You can compare it with the situation of closing and re-opening a desktop-based app.

Preserve state across circuits

Sometimes, it is required to preserve state across circuits as the app can retain user data when the server becomes unavailable or user browser force to start a new circuit for a new server. It is most important when a user actively play with data, not just reading existing data. You also need to think to store data in the other storage location rather than the data only stored on server memory to preserve the state beyond a single circuit. State persistence is not automatically done, but you must take care when you design the app for stateful data persistence.

Data persistence is more important when users have put effort in data creation. For example, in the shopping cart, a user has added many items to cart that he/she needs to purchase or with a multi-stage user info page, a user must enter much information in every page. If connection or state loss before the user submits data to the server for processing, the user needs to re-enter all the information.

Usually, it is not required to preserve the state that quickly recreated. For example, login page information, it is not necessary to persist the value of username in the text box.

Where to persist state

Depending on data, you can select a location for a persisting state in the Blazor server app. The following are prevalent locations where you can store the state.

- On Server in database
- On client in the browser
- URL

Base on scenario and requirement, you can select best-suited approaches.

On server in database

You can persist the state of the Blazor server app on the server in the database for data that need to be persisted for forever or span across multiple users. You can choose a relational database, Azure data storage, blob, or table storage, key-value storage to persist data. The new circuit is started by the user for any of the reasons; user data can be retrieved from the database, and it available for the new circuit.

On client in the browser

You can also persist in the user state in the browser's LocalStorage and SessionStorage. The main advantage of using client-side state management is you do not require to manage or clear the stored state when the circuit abandoned. There are few differences between LocalStorage and SessionStorage as following:

LocalStorage	SessionStorage
Its scoped to a user browser	Its scoped to a user browser tab
It persists state even if user reload or closes and re-opens browser page	It persists state only when the user reloads the browser page
It shares user state between multiple browser tabs	It maintains an independent version of the user state for every tab of browser
With LocalStorage, user state is persisted until explicitly cleared	With SessionStorage, the user state will be lost if browser tab or browser closed

Table 6.1: Comparison between local storage and session storage

The SessionStorage is an excellent way to persist state as LocalStorage shared state between multiple tabs, and sometimes behavior is confusing when multiple tabs overwrite user state. When an application needs to persist state across the tab or closing and re-opening the browser, the LocalStorage is the better choice.

URL

You can also persist in the state by sending small information in the URL. For Example, you can carry id of viewing entity or current page number of grid component in URL. It retained the user state when the user manually refreshes the page, but you cannot protect it from being modified.

Third-party browser storage solutions

NuGet provides the API that works with SessionStorage and LocalStorage. This API use ASP.NET core data protection that encrypts stored data hence reduce the risk of tampering stored data. If you stored the data in plain text JSON format, users could view and modify data using browser developer tools. It is recommended to store user sensitive data in encrypted form.

For Example, the NuGet package provides `DataProtection` for SessionStorage and LocalStorage using package `Microsoft.AspNetCore.ProtectedBrowserStorage`. Currently, it is in the experimental stage. However, you can also write your own service. This package internally uses JavaScript interop to store data into session or local storage. You can use this package by installing the package, add middleware and add package JavaScript to `_Host.cshtml` file.

You can also write your middleware that preserves data in either `SessionStorage` or LocalStorage. In the following example, it would be demonstrated how to create your middleware to preserve data in SessionStorage step by step:

1. Create a service that helps you to call the JavaScript interop to store data in windows session. This service contains three methods to get, add, and delete the value from the session. Each method makes JavaScript interop call to access the HTML windows session storage.

    Following is the code snippet of `ProtectedSessionStorage` service. Here, data protection is also added so, encrypted data stored in the session. The data is encrypted before it saves to session and decrypts after retrieves from the session.

    ```
    using System;
    using System.Collections.Concurrent;
    using System.Text.Json;
    using System.Threading.Tasks;
    using Microsoft.AspNetCore.DataProtection;
    using Microsoft.JSInterop;


    namespace StateManagement.Services
    ```

```
{
    public class ProtectedSessionStorage
    {
        private readonly static JsonSerializerOptions Serializer-
Options = new JsonSerializerOptions();
        private readonly IJSRuntime _jsRuntime;
        private readonly IDataProtectionProvider _dataProtection-
Provider;
        private readonly ConcurrentDictionary<string, IDataPro-
tector> _cachedDataProtectorsByPurpose
            = new ConcurrentDictionary<string, IDataProtector>();
        public ProtectedSessionStorage(IJSRuntime jsRuntime,
IDataProtectionProvider dataProtectionProvider)
        {
            _jsRuntime = jsRuntime ?? throw new ArgumentNullEx-
ception(nameof(jsRuntime));
            _dataProtectionProvider = dataProtectionProvider ??
throw new ArgumentNullException(nameof(dataProtectionProvider));
        }
        private IDataProtector GetOrCreateCachedProtector(string
purpose)
            => _cachedDataProtectorsByPurpose.GetOrAdd(
                purpose,
                _dataProtectionProvider.CreateProtector);

        public async ValueTask<T> GetAsync<T>(string key)
        {
            var protectedJson = await _jsRuntime.InvokeAsyn-
c<string>(
                $"ProtectedSessionStorage.get",
                key);

            if (protectedJson == null)
            {
                return default;
            }
```

```
            var protector = GetOrCreateCachedProtector(key);
            var json = protector.Unprotect(protectedJson);
            return JsonSerializer.Deserialize<T>(json, options:
    SerializerOptions);
        }
        public ValueTask SetAsync(string key, object value)
        {

            if (string.IsNullOrEmpty(key))
            {
                throw new ArgumentException("Cannot be null or
    empty", nameof(key));
            }

            var json = JsonSerializer.Serialize(value, options:
    SerializerOptions);

            var protector = GetOrCreateCachedProtector(key);
            var protectedJson = protector.Protect(json);
            return _jsRuntime.InvokeVoidAsync(
                $"ProtectedSessionStorage.set",
                key,
                protectedJson);
        }

        public ValueTask DeleteAsync(string key)
        {
            return _jsRuntime.InvokeVoidAsync(
                $"ProtectedSessionStorage.delete",
                key);
        }
    }
}
```

2. Write JavaScript that invoked by the C# method from service. Following is the code snippet of JavaScript. It looks straight forward, and it is only responsible to store, retrieve, and delete the data from the session. It stores data in session in key-value pair:

```
(function () {
    window.ProtectedSessionStorage = {
        get: (key) => window["SessionStorage"][key],
        set: (key, value) => { window["SessionStorage"][key] =
value; },
        delete: (key) => { delete window["SessionStorage"][key];
}
    };
})();
```

3. Register the service in `ConfigureService` method of `Startup` class (refer following code snippet):

```
public void ConfigureServices(IServiceCollection services)
{
    ...

    ...

    services.AddScoped<ProtectedSessionStorage>();

}
```

4. Register JavaScript file in top-level HTML file (`Pages/_Host.cshtml` for Blazor server app) using script tag (refer following code snippet):

```
<script src="~/ProtectedSessionStorage.js"></script>
```

Once, preceding defined steps are performed, your service is ready to use. To use the service in component, you must inject the service in component using `@inject` directive. In following code snippet, value of `currentCout` variable is stored as `SessionStorage['count']` in browser storage. Service encrypts the data before it stores it to the session, so, it does not store data in plain text. The service `SetAsync` method is used to stored data in session. Using service method `GetAsync` data recovered from session:

```
@page "/counter"

@using StateManagement.Services;

@inject ProtectedSessionStorage ProtectedSessionStore

<h1>Counter</h1>
```

```
<p>Current count: @currentCount</p>

<button class="btn btn-primary" @onclick="IncrementCount">Click me</button>

@code {
        int currentCount = 0;
    protected override async Task OnAfterRenderAsync(bool firstRender)
    {
        if (firstRender)
        {
            currentCount = await ProtectedSessionStore.GetAsync<int>("count");
            StateHasChanged();
        }
    }
    async Task IncrementCount()
    {
        currentCount++;
        await ProtectedSessionStore.SetAsync("count", currentCount);
    }
}
```

You can also verify data in browser storage (session storage); However, it is not in readable format and encrypted.(refer *Figure 6.1: How to check session storage in browser storage*).

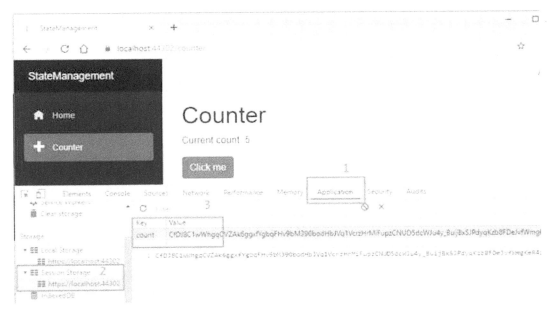

Figure 6.1: How to check session storage in browser storage

Similar way, you can create a service for local storage. In the pre-rendering event, the interactive connection between browser and server does not exist, so; the browser is not able to find the JavaScript that needs to run. It is the reason, Session **Storage** and **Local Storage** does not available in the pre-rendering event of the Blazor root component. It throws an error when the component is trying to access the storage. There is only one solution to resolve this error: do not access **Local Storage** or **Session Storage** in pre-rendering. It is the reason, OnAfterRenderAsync method is used to reload the state instead of the OnInitializedAsync method in the preceding example.

Summary

- Blazor is a stateful application. For the Blazor server app, the user state is stored in server memory and For Blazor client (WebAssembly) app, user state stored in client memory, and also, you can take advantage of client-side state management such as LocalStorage.

- When the Blazor server app is temporarily disconnected from the server due to any reason, it is trying to connect to the original circuit and app connecting back to the original state.

- The user receives a new connection circuit (with the empty state) when the app cannot connect with the original circuit.

- You may persist state in the following location:
    - o On Server in database
    - o On client in the browser
    - o URL
- Alternatively, you can use any third-party storage solution to persist in the state.

What you learned in this chapter?

In this chapter, you learned about state management and how to persist state for the Blazor server app and Blazor client app. This chapter also explained how to create your service to access client-side storage such as LocalStorage and SessionStorage.

What next?

In the next chapter, you will be learned about authentication and authorization with the Blazor app. You will also be learned about a different way to do authentication and authorization using third party services such as Google API and Facebook API.

Questions

1. What is the Blazor circuit?
2. What are the locations where the session can persist?
3. Is it possible to access JavaScript interop in the OnInitializedAsync method of the component?
4. Explain, how can you write middleware to persist state using LocalStorage and SessionStorage?

CHAPTER 7

Authentication and Authorization

Introduction

Authentication and authorization are the fundamental requirements of most of the applications. Authentication is a process to validate; the user has access to the application, and Authorization is a process to validate; the user has the right to access the application resource. Blazor uses the ASP.NET core security model to provide authentication and authorization. Both Blazor server app and client app (WebAssembly) have different security scenarios as Blazor server app uses server resource to provide authorization, and Blazor client app (WebAssembly) runs on the client; hence authorization is only determined which UI option can be accessible by the user.

In this chapter, we'll cover the following topics

- Authentication
  - o AuthenticationStateProvider service
  - o Custom AuthenticationStateProvider
- Authorization
  - o AuthorizeView
  - o Authorize attribute

       o   Custom content for unauthorized router component
- Authorization rules check-in procedural logic
- Authorization in Blazor client-side apps
- Authentication using third party service
  - Using Microsoft API
  - Using Google API
  - Using Facebook API
  - Use multiple authentication providers together

Objective
- Understand the basics of authentication and authorization
- Understand how to do authentication and authorization in Blazor server app and Blazor client app (WebAssembly)
- Understand how to do authentication and authorization using third-party services such as Google and Facebook API

Authentication

Blazor uses ASP.NET Core authentication mechanisms. It also depends on how the Blazor app is developed and host, Blazor server, or Blazor client (WebAssembly). Blazor server app uses SignalR for real-time connection between UI and server. SignalR is handled the authentication when connection established.

When you create the Blazor server project using the template, there is an option for setting up authentication for the project. The default authentication mode is none.

Following options are available to select authentication:
- No Authentication
- Individual User Accounts:
  - Using ASP.NET core Identity
  - using Azure AD B2C
- Work or School Accounts
- Windows authentication

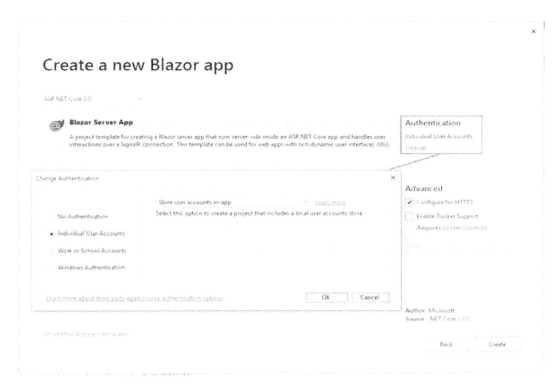

Figure 7.1: Change authentication option

The authentication in the Blazor client app (WebAssembly) can be bypassed as the user can modify the client-side code. It is true for all client-side frameworks such as Angular.

Blazor uses ASP.NET Core authentication mechanisms that support user interface for login functionality using the ASP.NET Core Identity membership system. You can create an account with login information that stored in identity or external login (such as Google, Microsoft, and Facebook account) can be used. You can configure identity using the SQL Server database to store user data such as name, password, and other profile data. ASP.NET Core provides UI for login functionality, and you can use one of the following to secure web apps:

- Azure Active Directory
- Azure Active Directory B2C (Azure AD B2C)
- IdentityServer4

When you want to use ASP.NET core identity with Blazor server app, select the **Individual User Accounts** option, as shown in *Figure 7.1: Change authentication option*. As a result, your application tracks the identity of the logged-in user. You can also apply authorization rules to users and roles.

When you run the application created by the Blazor server app template with an individual account, you find **Register** and **Login** option at top right corner as shown in *Figure 7.2: Output of Blazor server app with Individual account option:*

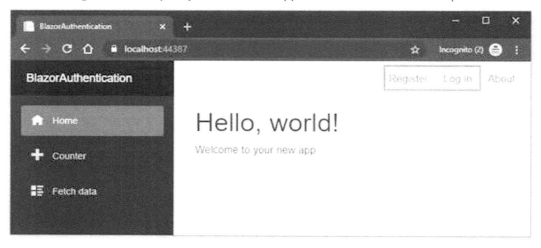

Figure 7.2: Output of Blazor server app with Individual account option

When you are accessing the database using this application and database does not exist, it allows you to migrate the database. The default connection string is stored in `appsettings.json` files.

After the migration, various tables are generated, related to the user and role management (refer *Figure 7.3: SQL query output after registration):*

Figure 7.3: SQL query output after registration

Here, the login page and registration page are not Blazor components, but they are Razor pages. These pages are injected using ASP.NET core identity middleware. When you look at `ConfigureServices` method of `Startup` class, you will find the following code:

```
services.AddDefaultIdentity<IdentityUser>();
```

This middleware adds a login and registration Razor component to the application; however, you can create your own components and use them.

AuthenticationStateProvider service

Blazor server app uses built-in `AuthenticationStateProvider` service. This service will find-out authentication state data from `HttpContext.User`. In this way, the Blazor server app uses ASP.NET Core existing authentication mechanisms. This service is used by `CascadingAuthenticationState` and `AuthorizeView` components to get the authentication states. With the Blazor server app, do not use `AuthenticationStateProvider` service directly as it does not notify automatically when authentication state data gets changed. That is the reason why it is recommended to use the `AuthorizeView` component.

In the following example code, `AuthenticationStateProvider` retrieves the user from ASP.NET Core's `HttpContext`. User and checks whether the user is authenticated or not. If the user is authenticated, it fetches user claims:

```
@page /
@using Microsoft.AspNetCore.Components.Authorization
@inject AuthenticationStateProvider AuthenticationStateProvider


<h1>Hello, world!</h1>


Welcome to your new app.


<p>
    @userAuthenticated
</p>


@code {
    string userAuthenticated;
    protected override async Task OnInitializedAsync()
    {
        var authState = await AuthenticationStateProvider.GetAuthentica-
tionStateAsync();
        var user = authState.User;
```

```
if (user.Identity.IsAuthenticated)
{
    userAuthenticated = ${user.Identity.Name} is authenticated.;
}
else
{
    userAuthenticated = The user is NOT authenticated.;
}
}
}
```

If IsAuthenticated property of the user.Identity is true; the user is authenticated else user is not authenticated (refer following *Figure 7.4: Blazor App output: before login and after login):*

Before Login

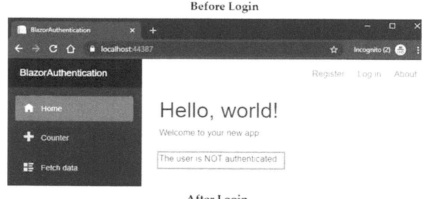

After Login

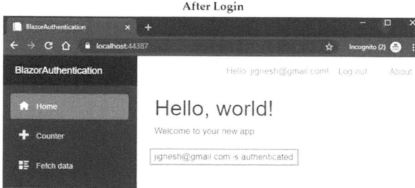

Figure 7.4: Blazor App output: before login and after login

The Blazor server app runs on the server; hence it able to fetch current user information from the server. With the Blazor client app, we need to configure custom `AuthenticationStateProvider` that fetches user information from the server by making an API call.

Custom AuthenticationStateProvider

The `AuthenticationStateProvider` service is built-in service in the Blazor server app that helps you to obtain the authentication state data from `HttpContext.User`. It is not very frequent scenario where you require to implement `CustomAuthenticationProvider`. The custom implementation may introduce security vulnerabilities to your app.

Blazor client-side (WebAssembly) can require a custom provider for `AuthenticationStateProvider` as you may want to integrate it with external authentication mechanisms that bypass server-side code. There are two easy steps to implement a custom `AuthenticationStateProvider`.

1. Create class that inherit from `AuthenticationStateProvider` abstract class and implement `GetAuthenticationStateAsync` abstract method (refer following code):

```
public class CustomAuthenticationStateProvider : Authentication-
StateProvider
{
    public override Task<AuthenticationState> GetAuthentication-
StateAsync()
    {
        var identity = new ClaimsIdentity(new[]
        {
            new Claim(ClaimTypes.Name, dummyName),
        }, Dummy authentication type);

        var user = new ClaimsPrincipal(identity);

        return Task.FromResult(new AuthenticationState(user));
    }
}
```

2. Register the custom authentication state provider in `ConfigureServices` method of startup class (refer following code):

```
services.AddScoped<AuthenticationStateProvider, CustomAuthentica-
tionStateProvider>();
```

When you use preceding custom authentication state providers, all users are authenticated with the dummyName users.

When you determine that authentication state data has changed for any reason such as user has logged out, then you can optionally call the NotifyAuthenticationStateChanged method of AuthenticationState Provider base class that notify all consumers of authentication state data such as AuthorizeView component.

Authorization

Authorization is a process to validate that uses has right to access the application resource. For example, the admin user can modify the system resource, but other users can only view the system resource. The authorization allows you to control user access to a resource based on roles, claims, and policies. The Blazor uses the same concept as ASP.NET Core uses for authentication and authorization. Authorization can be achieved in the Blazor app using an attribute, defined authorizations rule, and built-in component.

AuthorizeView

The Blazor app provides the AuthorizeView component that displays the page content, depending on user is authorized to see the content. It supports policy-based authorization and role-based authorization. This approach is beneficial when page content needs to display based on the role, policy, or authentication status of the user. You can access the AuthenticationState object using the context variable of the templated component.

In the following example code, the content under the AuthorizeView component is rendered if the user is authenticated. You can access user identity using context. User.Identity property:

```
<AuthorizeView>
    <h4>Hello, @context.User.Identity.Name!</h4>
    <p>This content is only visible if user is authenticated.</p>
</AuthorizeView>
```

With the AuthorizeView component, you can also define different content when the user is not authenticated. This component provides Authorized, and NotAuthorized render fragments. The Authorized fragment renders when the user is authenticated, and NotAuthorized fragment renders when the user is not authenticated. Both fragments accept other interactive components.

In the following example code, UI shows different text for authenticated and unauthenticated user:

```
<AuthorizeView>
    <Authorized>
        <h4>Hello, @context.User.Identity.Name!</h4>
        <p>This content is only visible if user is authenticated.</p>
    </Authorized>
    <NotAuthorized>
        <p>Please signed in.</p>
    </NotAuthorized>
</AuthorizeView>
```

`AuthorizeView` component uses default policies when authorization conditions are not defined. This component is also working with role-based, claim-based, and policy-based authorization.

The `AuthorizeView` component has the `Roles` parameter to perform do role-based authorization. In the following code example, page content is rendered based on roles:

```
<AuthorizeView Roles=Admin>
    <p>This content is only visible if user is in Admin role.</p>
</AuthorizeView>
<AuthorizeView Roles=User>
    <p>This content is only visible if user is in User role.</p>
</AuthorizeView>
```

Same way, the `AuthorizeView` component has the `Policy` parameter to perform policy-based authorization. In the following code example, page content is rendered only if policy conditions are satisfied.

```
<AuthorizeView Policy=OnlyAdminAccess>
    <p>This content is only visible if user is in Admin role.</p>
</AuthorizeView>
```

The claim-based authorization can be achieved using policy-based authorization. You can define a policy that checks for a particular claim. The default policy applies in `AuthorizeView` component if roles or policy is not specified.

The `AuthorizeView` provides Authorizing element to display content when authentication is in progress:

```
<AuthorizeView>
    <Authorizing>
        <h1>Authentication in progress</h1>
    </Authorizing>
</AuthorizeView>
```

Usually, the Blazor app knows its authentication state when the state is established, so content under the `Authorizing` element displays only when authorization is in progress.

Authorize attribute

The `AuthorizeView` component display UI depending on user authorization state. The `Authorize` attribute render Blazor component depending on user authorization state. The functionality of the `Authorize` attribute in the Blazor app is very similar to ASP.NET core. This attribute can be used with the `Razor` page as well as with the controller. The ASP.NET Core 3.0 introduced `@attribute` directive that helps you to define `Razor` page attribute in page component (refer following code snippet):

```
@page /home

@attribute [Authorize]
```

The `Authorize` attribute is applicable only if component reaches via a router. It does not perform authorization for the child components. `AuthorizeView` needs to be used instead of `Authorize` attribute for child component.

You can define `Authorize` attribute to page component or `_Imports.razor` page to apply authorization to all components under folder. It also supports role-based and policy-based authorization.

For role-based authorization, use `Roles` property and supplied a comma-separated list of roles that can access (refer following code snippet):

```
@page /home

@attribute [Authorize(Roles = admin, HR)]
```

For policy-based authorization, use `Policy` property and supplied a comma-separated list of policy that can access (refer following code snippet):

```
@page /home

@attribute [Authorize(Policy = OnlyAdminAccess)]
```

The default policy is applied in Authorize attribute if roles or policy is not specified.

Custom content for unauthorized router component

The route component allows you to specify custom content when the user is not authorized; authorization is in progress and content not found. This component provides <NotFound>, <NotAuthorized>, and <Authorizing> render fragment to specify custom content. The custom content can be added to the app.razor file. The NotAuthorized and Authorizing tags must specify under AuthorizeRouteView tags. If you do not specify NotAuthorized element, Blazor app shows default message:

```
<Router AppAssembly=@typeof(Program).Assembly>

    <Found Context=routeData>

        <AuthorizeRouteView RouteData=@routeData DefaultLayout=@typeof(-
MainLayout)>

            <NotAuthorized>

                <h4>Not authorized.</h4>

            </NotAuthorized>

            <Authorizing>

                <h4>Authentication in progress...</h4>

            </Authorizing>

        </AuthorizeRouteView>

    </Found>

    <NotFound>

        <CascadingAuthenticationState>

            <LayoutView Layout=@typeof(MainLayout)>

                <p>Sorry, there's nothing at this address.</p>

            </LayoutView>

        </CascadingAuthenticationState>

    </NotFound>

</Router>
```

You can also include arbitrary items such as interactive components under <NotFound>, <NotAuthorized>, and <Authorizing> tags.

Authorization rules check-in procedural logic

Sometimes, you required to check for authorization as part of procedural logic. You can retrieve the user authentication state using `AuthenticationStateProvider` (as describes earlier). Here, you must retrieve the user authentication state whenever you required. Alternatively, you can pass the user authentication state using the cascaded parameter of type `Task<AuthenticationState>`.

In the following code snippet, `authenticationStateTask` property (a type of `Task<AuthenticationState>`) defined as a `CascadingParameter`, and you can retrieve user info from User property of `authenticationStateTask`:

```
@code {

    [CascadingParameter]
    Task<AuthenticationState> authenticationStateTask { get; set; }

    string message = string.Empty;

    protected override async Task OnInitializedAsync()
    {
        var user = (await authenticationStateTask).User;

        if (user.Identity.IsAuthenticated)
        {
            message += User is Authenticated. ;
        }

        if (user.IsInRole(admin))
        {
            message += User is in Admin role.;
        }
    }
}
```

You can also use this cascading parameter in `AuthorizeRouteView` using `CascadingAuthenticationState` components.

Authorization in Blazor client-side apps

In the Blazor server app, the app is running on the server, so authorization checks cannot bypass. But in the Blazor client app (WebAssembly), code is running on the client browser and can be modified by the user and authorization can be bypassed. You must perform an authorization check on the server for any API call from the Blazor client app. It is true for all client-side frameworks, including the JavaScript SPA framework.

Authentication using third party service

The Blazor use ASP.NET core authentication mechanisms, and ASP.NET Core allows user to sign-in with external authentication providers such as Google, Facebook, Twitter, and Microsoft. The third-party authentication feature enables the user to use their existing credentials. You need to pass some of the original request information such as secure request scheme (https), host, and client IP address to app request header when app deploys behind a load balancer or proxy server. The secure request scheme is used to generate an authentication link with the external provider. If you are not passing the correct secure scheme, it generates an incorrect return URL.

If you want to use third-party service for authentication, you need to create a respective social app, and the social app provides you the `Application Id` and `Application Secret` tokens that use to access a social app to verify the user. Once you get the application id and secret, you can store it to configuration files such as `appsettings.json`.

Using Microsoft API

To do authentication using the Microsoft developer portal, you must register the app and link it to your Microsoft account. If you did not have a Microsoft account, create one. The following are the steps to register the app to Microsoft account.

1. Navigate to URL: **https://go.microsoft.com/fwlink/?linkid=2083908**

   Login with your existing Microsoft account credential or create a new account. It validates the credential and redirects to the Azure portal's App registrations page. Click on **New registration** button (refer *Figure 7.5: Microsoft account – new project registration*):

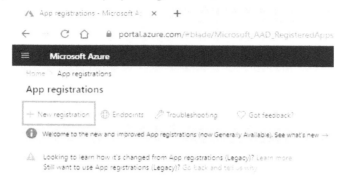

Figure 7.5: *Microsoft account – new project registration*

2. Fill up required filed on the form such as **Name**, supported account types and redirect to URI and click on **Register** button (refer *Figure 7.6: Microsoft account – registration page*):

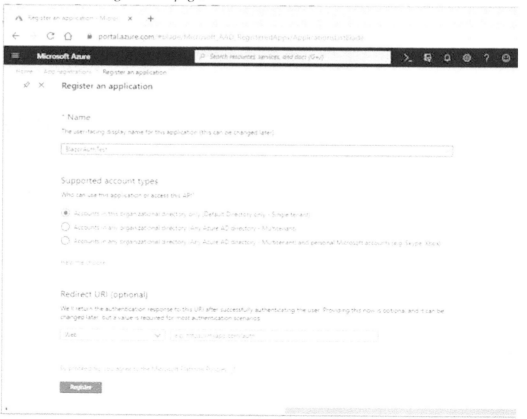

Figure 7.6: *Microsoft account – registration page*

It will create the app on the Azure portal and provide you client ID (application) and talent (directory) id.

3. Create a client secret. To create client secret, click on **Certificates & secrets** from the left panel (refer *Figure 7.6: Microsoft account – registration page):*

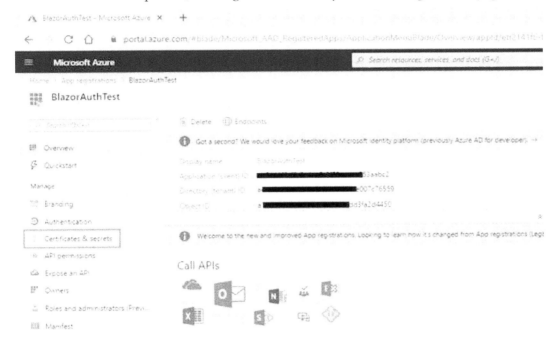

Figure 7.7: *Microsoft account – after initial registration*

Under **Client secrets** pane, click on the **New client secret** button. It will pop the dialog box that allows you to add client secret description and secret expiry (refer *Figure 7.8: Microsoft account – create client secret),* and then, click on the **Add** button.

It will generate the client secret that can be used along with client ID for authentication:

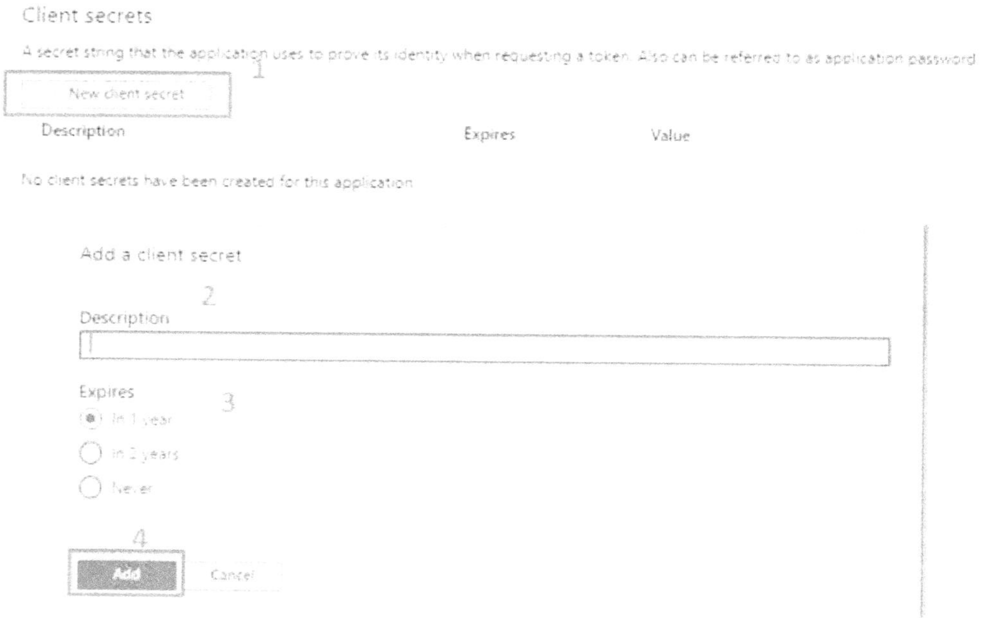

Figure 7.8: Microsoft account – create a client secret

The next step is to configure Microsoft authentication in your project, and the following are the steps to configure Microsoft authentication in the Blazor server project.

1. The first step is to create a Blazor server app using a Visual Studio template with an individual user account option.

2. The next step is to install Microsoft authentication middleware using the NuGet package manager. The following code shows the command to install this middleware that needs to run in the NuGet package manager console. This NuGet package adds `AddMicrosoftAccount` extension method:

   ```
   Install-Package Microsoft.AspNetCore.Authentication.
   MicrosoftAccount
   ```

3. The next step is to configure Microsoft account authentication middleware in the `ConfigureService` method of startup class using the `AddMicrosoftAccount` extension method. Here, you must pass the client ID and secret that you get by following the steps in the preceding section. The best practice is to store this client ID and secret in the configuration file (any of JSON file such as `appsettings.json`). Following code shows the structure of the configuration file:

```
    {
      Authentication: {
        Microsoft: {
          ClientId: client Id,
          ClientSecret: Client secret
        }
      }
    }
```

Following code is required to configure Microsoft account authentication middle ware in your project:

```
services.AddAuthentication().AddMicrosoftAccount(microsoftOptions =>
{
    microsoftOptions.ClientId = Configuration[Authentication:Microsoft:-
ClientId];
    microsoftOptions.ClientSecret = Configuration[Authentication:Micro-
soft:ClientSecret];
});
```

The Microsoft account authentication middleware adds **Microsoft** button in both registration and login page (refer following *Figure 7.9: Microsoft account – login option*).

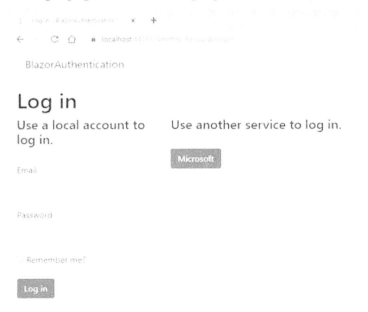

Figure 7.9: Microsoft account – login option

When you click on the **Microsoft** button, the page is redirected to the Microsoft login page (refer *Figure 7.10: Microsoft account – redirect to Microsoft login page)*, and if authentication is get done successfully, it redirects to return URL that supplied at the time of new registration page.

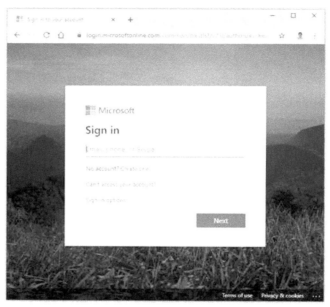

Figure 7.10: *Microsoft account – redirect to Microsoft login page*

You can modify callback URI when Microsoft account authentication middleware is configured. Set new callback URI to `RemoteAuthenticationOptions.CallbackPath` property of the `MicrosoftAccountOptions class`.

Using Google API

To do authentication using Google API, you must create a Google API console project that provides client id and secret. This client id and secret use to configure authentication in your project. The following are the steps to create a Google project.

1. Navigate to URL: **https://developers.google.com/identity/sign-in/web/sign-in#before_you_begin**

Login with your existing google account credential or create a new account and then click on **Configure a Project** button (refer *Figure 7.11: Google – configure project):*

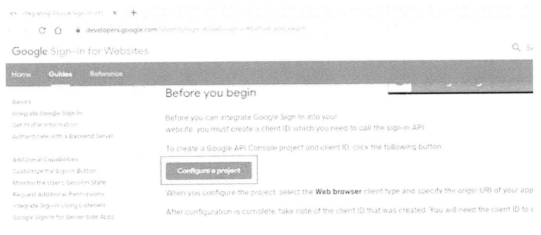

Figure 7.11: Google – configure the project

2. It navigates to **Configure a project** for Google Sign-in dialog box. Here, it required to provide a project name. Alternatively, you can also select an existing project (associated with your log in account) from the dropdown. Click on next button to navigate to next screen (refer *Figure 7.12: Google – Create a new project or select existing one):*

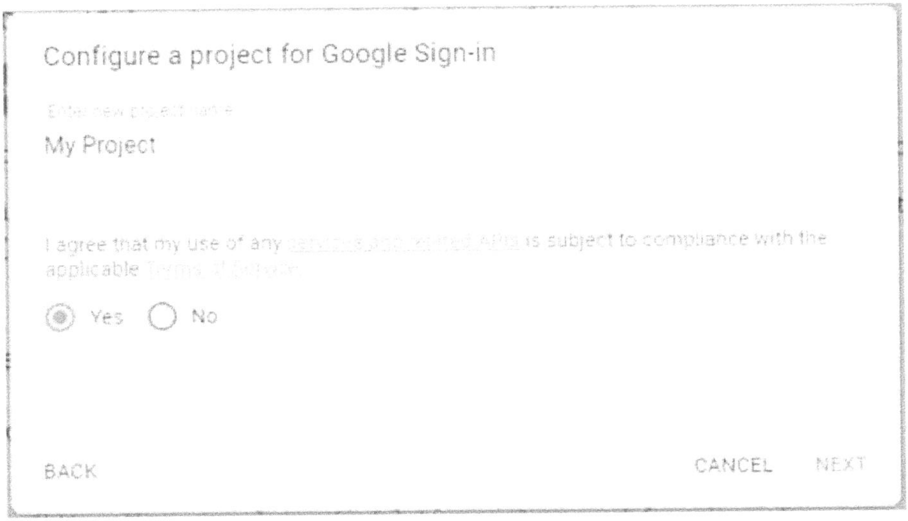

Configure a project for Google Sign-in

My Project

I agree that my use of any related APIs is subject to compliance with the applicable Terms of Service.

⦿ Yes   ◯ No

BACK   CANCEL   NEXT

Figure 7.12: Google – Create a new project or select existing one

Do not use word Google in your **Project** and **Product** name as it is a prohibited word, and both must be between 4 and 30 characters.

3. Now, it navigates to **Configure your OAuth client** dialog box. Here, you need to provide a product name. Click on the **NEXT** button to navigate to the next screen (refer *Figure 7.12: Google – Create a new project or select existing one*).

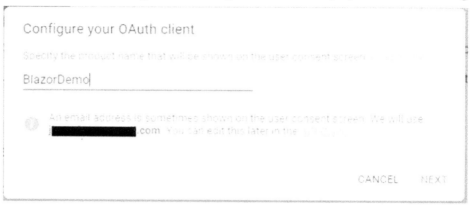

Figure 7.13: Google – configure the client

4. In the next screen, you need to select from where you are `supposed to call this` Google API. For the Blazor app, you need to select a web server from the options. Also, you need to provide **Authorized redirect URIs.** It is base URL with /sign in-google appended text and clicks on **Create** button(refer *Figure 7.12: Google – Create a new project or select existing one*):

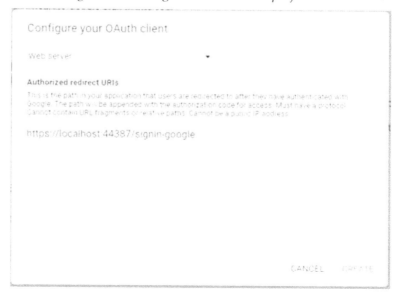

Figure 7.14: Google – configure redirect URI

5. Now almost done for Google project and provides you a **Client ID** and **Client Secret** that uses in google account authentication (refer *Figure 7.15: Google – provide client Id and secret*):

Figure 7.15: Google – provide client Id and secret

The next step is to configure Google authentication in your project, and the following are the steps to configure Google authentication in the Blazor server project.

1. The first step is to create the Blazor server app using a Visual Studio template with an individual user account option.

2. The next step is to install Google authentication middleware using the NuGet package manager. The following code shows the command to install this middleware that needs to run in the NuGet package manager console. This NuGet package adds AddGoogle extension method:

```
PM> Install-Package Microsoft.AspNetCore.Authentication.Google
```

3. The next step is to configure Google authentication middleware in the `ConfigureService` method of startup class using the `AddGoogle` extension method. Here, you must pass the client ID and secret that you get by following the steps in the preceding section. The best practice is to store this client id and secret in the configuration file (any of JSON file such as `appsettings.json`). Following code shows the structure of the configuration file:

```
{
  Authentication: {
    Google: {
      ClientId: client Id,
```

```
        ClientSecret: Client secret
     }
   }
 }
```

Following code is required to configure Google authentication middleware in your project:

```
public void ConfigureServices(IServiceCollection services)
{
    ...

    ...

    services.AddAuthentication()
    .AddGoogle(googleOptions =>
    {
        googleOptions.ClientId = Configuration[Authentication:Google:Cli-
entId];

        googleOptions.ClientSecret = Configuration[Authentication:Google:-
ClientSecret];
    });
}
```

The Google authentication middleware adds **Google** button in both registration and login page (refer following *Figure 7.16: Google login option):*

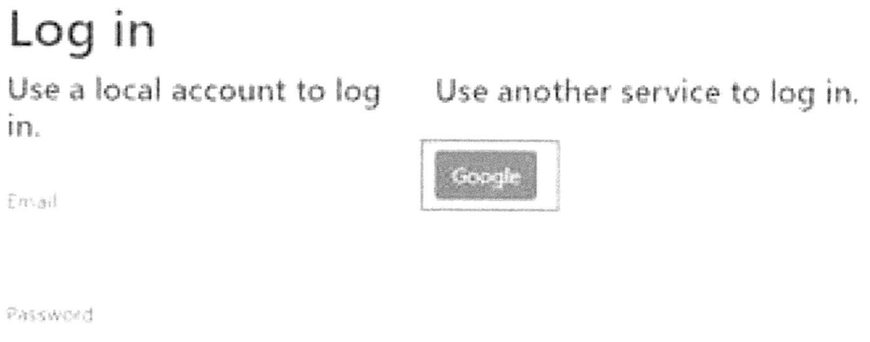

Figure 7.16: Google login option

When you click on the **Google** button, the page is redirected to the Google login page (refer *Figure 7.16: Google login option*). If authentication is get done successfully, it redirects to return URL that supplied at the time of Google project setup:

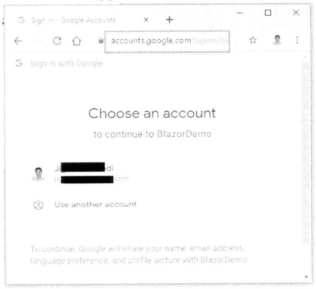

Figure 7.17: *Google – redirect to Google login page*

You can modify callback URI when Google authentication middleware is configured. Set new callback URI to `RemoteAuthenticationOptions.CallbackPath` property of the `GoogleOptions` class.

Using Facebook API

To setup Facebook authentication, you must create an app project that provides app ID and secret. This app ID and secret use to configure authentication in your project. The following are the steps to create an app using Facebook API.

1. Navigate to URL: **https://developers.facebook.com/apps/**

   Login with your existing Facebook account credential or create a new account. If your account is not registered with the Facebook developer, then you need to register (refer the *Figure 7.18: Facebook – Become Facebook Developer*):

Figure 7.18: *Facebook – Become Facebook Developer*

2. **Create App.** Once you become a Facebook developer, it allows you to create an app (refer to *Figure 7.18: Facebook – Become Facebook Developer*):

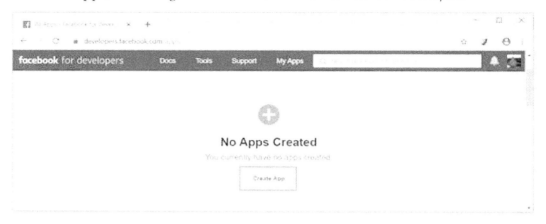

Figure 7.19: Facebook – Create an app on Facebook

When you click on **Create App** button, it is asking some mandatory details such as app display name and contact email. Click **Create App ID** button to create App Id (refer *Figure 7.20: Facebook – Create app Id*):

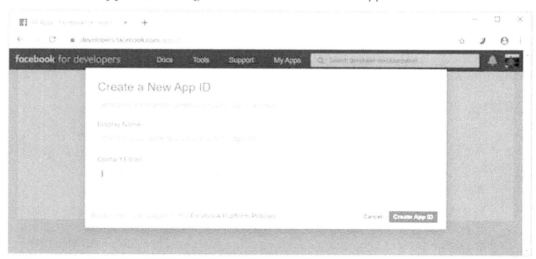

Figure 7.20: Facebook – Create app Id

3. Setup **Facebook Login**. To setup Facebook login, click on the **Set Up** button on **Facebook Login** card (refer *Figure 7.21: Facebook – Set up Facebook login*). It redirects to the quick start menu:

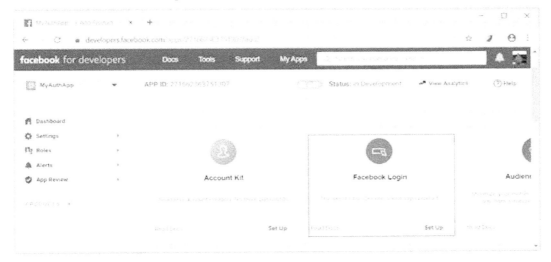

Figure 7.21: *Facebook – Set up Facebook login*

In the quick start option, it is asking for which kind of application use this Facebook login. For Blazor server app, you need to select the **WWW (Web)** app (refer *Figure 7.21: Facebook – Set up Facebook login)*:

Figure 7.22: *Facebook – Quickstart menu*

Here, you need to pass the Site URL that accesses the Facebook page for authentication (refer *Figure 7.23: Facebook – Setup Web app in Facebook login*). This page also contains the other setting, and every setting has its own save button.

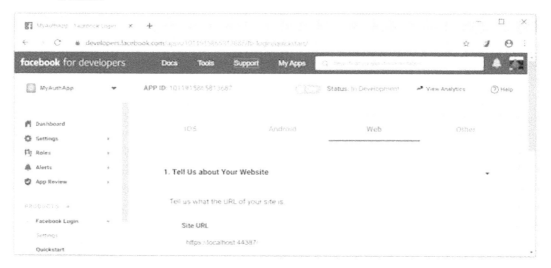

Figure 7.23: *Facebook – Setup Web app in Facebook login*

4. Get **App ID** and **App Secret.** You can get app id and secret from **Setting > Basic** tab (refer *Figure 7.24: Facebook – Get App Id and Secret*). From here, you can modify other details such as app domains, contact email, and so on:

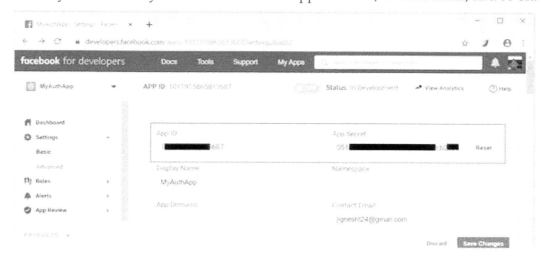

Figure 7.24: *Facebook – Get App Id and Secret*

This app id and secret use for authentication Blazor App. The next step is to configure Google authentication in your project, and the following are the steps to configure Google authentication in the Blazor server project.

1. The first step is to create the Blazor server app using the Visual Studio template with an individual user account option.

2. The next step is to install Facebook authentication middleware using the NuGet package manager. The following code shows the command to install this middleware that needs to run in the NuGet package manager console. This NuGet package adds the `AddFacebook` extension method.

```
PM> Install-Package Microsoft.AspNetCore.Authentication.Facebook
```

3. The next step is to configure Facebook authentication middleware in the `ConfigureService` method of startup class using the `AddFacebook` extension method. Here, you must pass the AppId and secret that you get by following the steps in the preceding section. The best practice is to store this app id and secret in the configuration file (any of JSON files such as `appsettings.json`). Following code shows the structure of the configuration file:

```
{
  Authentication: {
    Facebook: {
      AppId: App Id,
      AppSecret: App secret
    }
  }
}
```

Following code is required to configure Facebook authentication middle ware in your project:

```
public void ConfigureServices(IServiceCollection services)
{
    ...

    ...

    services.AddAuthentication()
        .AddFacebook(facebookOptions =>
    {
        facebookOptions.AppId = Configuration[Authentication:Facebook:AppId];
        facebookOptions.AppSecret = Configuration[Authentication:Face-
```

```
book:AppSecret];
    });
}
```

The Facebook authentication middleware adds the **Facebook** button in both registration and login page (refer following *Figure 7.25: Facebook login option*):

Log in

Use a local account to log in.

Use another service to log in.

Facebook

Email

Password

Remember me!

Log in

Figure 7.25: Facebook login option

When you click on the **Facebook** button, the page is redirected to the Facebook login page (refer *Figure 7.26: Facebook – redirect to the Facebook login page*), and if authentication is get done successfully, it redirects to return URL:

Figure 7.26: Facebook – redirect to the Facebook login page

You can modify callback URI when Facebook authentication middleware is configured. Set new callback URI to `RemoteAuthenticationOptions.CallbackPath` property of the `FacebookOptions` class.

Use multiple authentication providers together

You can also add multiple third-party authentication providers to your Blazor server app. IT can be achieved by chaining the provider extension after the `AddAuthentication` method in the `configureService` method of `Startup` class.

In the following code snippet, four third-party (Microsoft account, Google, Facebook, and Twitter) authentication providers are added:

```
services.AddAuthentication()
    .AddMicrosoftAccount(microsoftOptions => { ... })
    .AddGoogle(googleOptions => { ... })
    .AddFacebook(facebookOptions => { ... })
    .AddTwitter(twitterOptions => { ... });
```

When you run the application, all four providers button will be visible, and you can perform the authentication using any one of them (refer *Figure 7.27: Multiple authentication provider option):*

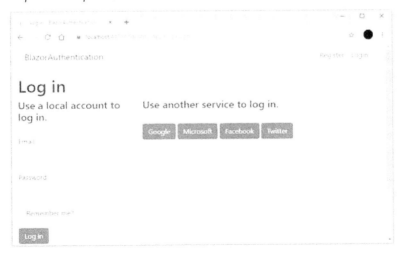

Figure 7.27: Multiple authentication provider option

The sequence of the provider login button is the same as the sequence as you register the middleware for the providers.

When you are login with the external provider, and you are not registered the user for an app, the app is asking for register the user, and the **Register** button is visible on the page (refer *Figure 7.28: Registration for external users*). It is applied to all external providers.

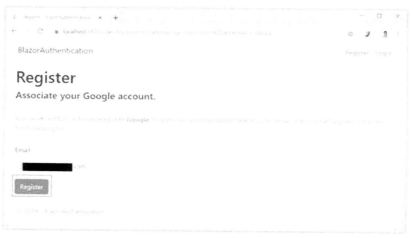

Figure 7.28: Registration for external users

It is not required a password to register the user in the app when you register with external login. When the external login provider is unavailable, or you do not have an internet connection, you cannot log in to the app.

Summary

- Authentication is a process to validate; the user has access to the application, and Authorization is a process to validate; the user has the right to access the application resource.

- Blazor use ASP.NET core authentication and authorization mechanisms

- You can use built-in `AuthenticationStateProvider` service to access user identity.

- You can also write a custom `AuthenticationStateProvider` server for your app, but it is not recommended as it introduces security vulnerabilities.

- Blazor provides `AuthorizeView` component that displays the content based on user authentication and authorization state:

  o It provides Authorized, and `NotAuthorized` render fragments that display content when the user is authenticated or not authenticated, respectively.

  o Using the `Role` parameter, you can do roles-based authorization.

  o Using the `Policy` parameter, you can do policy-based authorization.

o Using the `Authorizing` element, you can display the content when authentication is in progress.

- The `Authorize` attribute render Blazor component depending on user authorization state:

    o You can define Authorize attribute in Blazor component using `@attribute` directive.

    o The `Authorize` attribute applicable only if component reaches via a router. It does not perform authorization for the child component.

    o When you define, `Authorize` attribute to `_Imports.razor` page that applied authorization to all components under folder.

    o You can also do role-based and policy-based authorization using the `Authorize` attribute.

- Blazor allows users to sign-in with external authentication providers such as Google, Facebook, Twitter, and Microsoft.

- You can also add multiple external authentication providers to your Blazor server app.

What you learned in this chapter?

In this chapter, you learn about how to do authentication and authorization in the Blazor server app, learn about the various Blazor component such as AuthorizeView and Authorize attribute and learn about how to do authentication using external providers such as Google, Facebook, Twitter, and Microsoft.

What next?

In the next chapter, you will be learned about how to handle the exception in the Blazor app and how to use a built-in logging framework to log the exception. It also explains about 3rd party logging framework providers such as serilog.

Questions

1. What are authentication and authorization?

2. What is the use of AuthenticationStateProvider service?

3. How can you access the user identity using AuthenticationStateProvider service?

4. What is the use of the AuthorizeView component?

5. Describe the features of the AuthorizeView component?

6. What is the use of the Authorize attribute?

7. How can you do authentication using external providers such as Google, Facebook, and so on?

CHAPTER 8
Handle Exception and Log Error

Introduction

The exception is an unexpected error condition occured while executing the code. Most of the exception occur due to logical and technical errors in code. Handling the exception is essential for every application as it allows code defensively and minimizes the chance of crashing. Another essential point is logging the exceptions in any storage so that administrator users can analyze the exception the take appropriate action.

There are multiple reasons and places where the exception can arise, and there are multiple ways to handle the exceptions. In this chapter, you will learn about the place where the exceptions can generate and different ways to handle and log the exceptions.

In this chapter, we'll cover the following topics

- The behavior of Blazor app for an unhandled exceptions
- Places where errors may occur
- Introduction to the logging framework
- Configure logging provider
- Logging using serilog

Objective

- Understand how to handle the exception
- Understand the logging framework

The behavior of Blazor app for an unhandled exception

As you learned in the previous chapter, the Blazor server is a stateful application framework, so it maintains the connection to the server. It is generally known as the Blazor circuit. The Blazor circuit holds many essential items such as active component instance, most recent rendered components, and event handling delegates. Blazor creates a separate circuit for each user browser connection, so when the user opens multiple tabs, there are multiple circuits. All the circuit works independently.

Every unhandled exception considers as fatal to the circuit for the Blazor server app. For some of the unhandled exceptions, the Blazor app terminates the circuit, so the user needs to reload the page to create a new circuit, and the existing circuit cannot be retrieved. All the circuit work independently, so terminated circuits don't affect any other circuits. You can compare the scenario with the desktop app as desktop app crashes, and it must restart to continue work.

You must need to add suitable exception handling logic to the app to continue work with the app (without interrupt) after an exception is generated.

Places where errors may occur

Following are some places where an error may occur while executing your code:

Component instantiation

When the component is initialized by Blazor, it invokes constructor and then trying to retrieve the service instance that supplied in the constructor using @inject directive or [Inject] attribute. If any error occurred in the constructor or setting service instance to local property, the framework can't load the component.

Lifecycle methods

During the component initialization, Blazor invoked various life cycle events such as OnInitialized / OnInitializedAsync, OnParametersSet / OnParameters SetAsync, ShouldRender / ShouldRenderAsync and OnAfterRender / OnAfter RenderAsync. If any exception occurred during the execution of any life cycle event, it is fatal to the circuit, and Blazor do not understand how to load the component.

Rendering logic

Blazor framework generates the `BlazorRenderTree` for the component when it renders, and during this time, data binding and element rendering are happening. Render logic may throw the exception when the model is not initialized, or some of the properties are null and trying to access internal properties. It is fatal to the circuit.

Component disposal

The component can implement the `System.IDisposable` interface and abstract method Dispose called when the user is navigated to one page to another page. The dispose logic may throw an exception. It is also fatal for the circuit. You can use a try-catch block when you know that your code can fail for any reason when the component disposed.

JavaScript interop

Blazor supports the JavaScript interop that allows you to call JavaScript function from C# code and vice-versa. The JavaScript interop call can generate the unhandled exception when supplied arguments are not serialized, and Server-side / client-side code may have unexpected value, the invalid parameter value of the method, and so on. When C# code thrown the unhandled exception, it does not treat as fatal for the circuit because of this misbehaving in JavaScript code.

Event handlers

Blazor invoked the C# code when an event has occurred. It might possible underlying code in the event handler is generated an unhandled exception. It is fatal to the circuit. You can use a try-catch block when you know that your code can fail for any reason.

Circuit handlers and disposal

The circuit handler allows you to write code in a particular state of user circuit such as initialized, connected, disconnected, and disposed of. This notification managed by the `CircuitHandler` service that registers using DI. When the circuit handler method throws the unhandled exception, this is fatal to the circuit.

Prerendering

When the page in Blazor app render, components are also rendered at that time. The component use `RenderComponentAsync<TComponent>` extension method of HTML helper for pre-rendering. Any exception occurred the pre-rendering, this is fatal to the circuit, and there is no meaning to render this component as it does not work.

Enabling detailed errors

When an unhandled exception occurred, the Blazor server app disconnects the circuit and adds an exception in the browser console. However, it is not a detailed error as the end-user does not require detail about the exception. When an unhandled exception occurred, the high-level, Blazor only shows that exception occurred but not provide any details (refer *Figure 8.1: Unhandled exception browser console):*

Figure 8.1: Unhandled exception browser console

In the development environment, it is required a detailed error for debugging purposes. Blazor provides an option to enable detailed errors that provides you most useful information about the exception.

You can enable detailed error by setting up `DetailedErrors` property of circuit option to true. You can add circuit option using `AddCircuitOptions` extension method just after `AddServerSideBlazor` method in configure method of startup class (refer following code snippet):

```
public void ConfigureServices(IServiceCollection services)
{
    ...

    services.AddServerSideBlazor()
        .AddCircuitOptions(options => { options.DetailedErrors = true;
});
    ...

    ...
```

```
}
```

Blazor app enables you to display detail error in the browser console when an exception occurred (refer *Figure 8.2: Detail of exception in browser console)*:

Figure 8.2: Detail of exception in the browser console

The current version of Blazor does not provide costly exception handling, and it does not use the ASP.NET Core exception handling mechanism once the circuit is established. So, you must use a try-catch block to handle the exception. The `catch` block catches the exception, and you can log the exception in file or database and show an appropriate message to the user:

```
try
{
    //Write your code that might generate exception.
}
catch(Exception ex)
{

}
```

So, you need to write a try-catch block in every code block that might generate an exception.

Introduction to the logging framework

Logging the exception is an essential part as it helps you to debug code and investigate the problem in logic. The ASP.NET core has built-in support for the logging framework, and there are extensions available for the Blazor app that help you to log the exceptions. These extensions are the implementation of `Microsoft.Extensions.Logging` to support the `ILogger` interface. This extension provides the same features as `Microsoft.Extensions.Logging` provides for .NET Core.

Configure logging provider

The logging extensions are not coming with the default Blazor server app template so, you need to configure logging extension in the Blazor project. The extensions are available on the NuGet. You can add a logging extensions to the Blazor project using the NuGet package manager or .NET core CLI. Following command is used to add an extension to Blazor project using NuGet package manager:

```
PM> Install-Package Blazor.Extensions.Logging -Version 1.0.0
```

The next step is to register the logging extension. There are different extension methods available to configure different types of logging; for example, the `AddBrowserConsole` method use to configure browser console logger. Using the following code, you can set up the browser console logger for the Blazor app:

```
public void ConfigureServices(IServiceCollection services)
{
    ...

    services.AddLogging(builder => builder
        .AddBrowserConsole()
        .SetMinimumLevel(LogLevel.Trace)
        );

    ...

}
```

To consume a logger in the Blazor component, you need to inject ILogger service to the component. There are various extension methods available to log the message. For example, `LogDebug` method uses to format and write a debug log message (refer following code snippet):

```
@page "/"

@inject ILogger<Index> logger

<h1>Hello, world!</h1>

Welcome to your new app.

@code{
    protected override async Task OnInitializedAsync()
    {
        logger.LogDebug("Component init");
    }
```

}

The logging framework provides built-in extension methods based on the log level. Following log levels supported by logging framework:

- Trace
- Debug
- Information
- Warning
- Error
- Critical
- None

For example, to log information, you can use the `LogInformation` extension method.

Set default minimum log level

You can set the minimum log level using the `SetMinimumLevel` method of the `LoggingBuilderExtensions` class. It sets a minimum logging level for log messages. The log level below the minimum log level is ignored. The default minimum logging level is `information`; hence `Debug` and `Trace` are ignored.

Following code used to set the minimum log level to `Warning`, so only `Warning`, `Error` and `Critical` log messages are logged:

```
services.AddLogging(builder => builder
    .AddBrowserConsole()
    .SetMinimumLevel(LogLevel.Warning)
    );
```

Blazor logging extension provides nearly the same features as **Microsoft Extensions Logging (MEL)** provides. You can also use third-party logging providers such as serilog, elmah.io, and so on.

Logging using serilog

The serilog provides diagnostic logging to various places such as console, file, and so on. It is easy to implement and highly configurable. The serilog provides various sinks to log to various platforms such as browser console, file, MSSQL, and so on.

The configuration of serilog is quite easy and slightly different from the built-in logging provider configuration. You need to configure serilog in the `Program class`.

The `CreateLogger` extension method of the `LoggerConfiguration` class creates a logger instance using configured sinks and another configuration. The Blazor client project supports log to write to the browser console. Blazor server project supports many options for logging, and it very similar to the ASP.NET Core application.

For the client app, you need to install browser console sink (`Serilog.Sinks.BrowserConsole`) using the NuGet package manager or Core CLI. This sink provides method `BrowserConsole` that enabled write log in the browser console. Following code snippet shows serilog configuration for logging to the browser console:

```
public class Program
{
    public static void Main(string[] args)
    {
        Log.Logger = new LoggerConfiguration()
            .Enrich.WithProperty("InstanceId", Guid.NewGuid().To-
String("n"))
            .WriteTo.BrowserConsole()
            .CreateLogger();
        try
        {
            Log.Information("Starting up");
            CreateHostBuilder(args).Build().Run();
        }
        catch (Exception ex)
        {
            Log.Fatal(ex, "Application start-up failed");
        }
        finally
        {
            Log.CloseAndFlush();
        }
    }
    public static IHostBuilder CreateHostBuilder(string[] args) =>
        Host.CreateDefaultBuilder(args)
            .ConfigureWebHostDefaults(webBuilder =>
```

```
        {
            webBuilder.UseStartup<Startup>();
        })
    ;
}
```

The `CloseAndFlush` method of Log class reset logger to default and try to dispose of the original logger object. The `WriteTo.BrowserConsole` method writes log event to the browser console. It will only work with the Blazor client project.

The Logging using serilog in the Blazor server project is very similar to logging in the ASP.NET Core app. For the Blazor server project, serilog provides various sinks to write log in the file, database, and so on.

The first step to configure serilog in the Blazor server project is to install `Serilog.AspNetCore`. You can install this package either using the NuGet package manager or dotnet CLI. Using the following command, you can install this package to the Blazor server project using dotnet CLI.

```
> dotnet add package Serilog.AspNetCore
```

The next step is to configure serilog in the `Program` class. It is very similar to the configuration in the Blazor client project but additionally set serilog as a logging service provider using `UseSerilog` method:

```
public class Program
{
    public static void Main(string[] args)
    {
        Log.Logger = new LoggerConfiguration()
            .Enrich.FromLogContext()
            .WriteTo.Console()
            .CreateLogger();
        try
        {
            Log.Information("Starting up");
            CreateHostBuilder(args).Build().Run();
        }
        catch (Exception ex)
        {
```

```
            Log.Fatal(ex, "Application start-up failed");
        }
        finally
        {
            Log.CloseAndFlush();
        }
    }
    public static IHostBuilder CreateHostBuilder(string[] args) =>
        Host.CreateDefaultBuilder(args)
            .UseSerilog()
            .ConfigureWebHostDefaults(webBuilder =>
            {
                webBuilder.UseStartup<Startup>();
            })
        ;
}
```

For the Blazor server project, `WriteTo.Console` method does not write log in browser console but server command console (refer *Figure 8.3: command prompt console*):

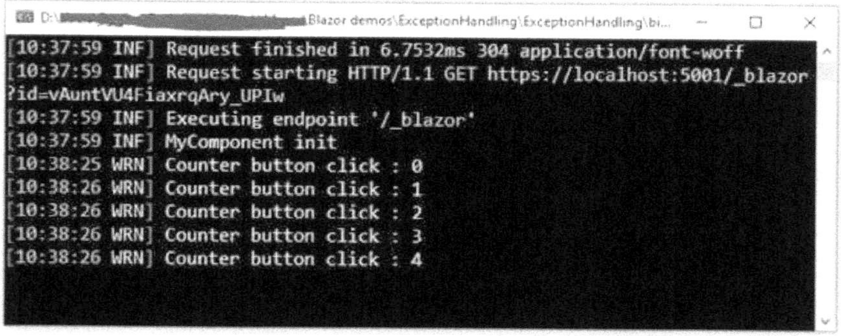

Figure 8.3: command prompt console

The serilog does not use the logging section of the `appSetting.json` file. If you use serilog as a logging provider, you can remove this section from the `appSetting.json` file.

Write log to file using serilog

The serilog provides file sinks as default sinks. To write a log to file, you don't need to install an additional sink, but you need to do some additional configuration. The serilog sink provides `WriteTo.File` method that use to write log to file. The file will be written using the UTF-8-character set to provide the location.

Following code snippet shows configuration of file sink that write log file to specified location:

```
Log.Logger = new LoggerConfiguration()
         .Enrich.FromLogContext()
         .WriteTo.File(@"C:\logs\log.txt")
.CreateLogger();
```

The serilog is highly configurable. It provides various option for configuring such as:

- It allows specifying rolling interval and size
- It allows specifying output template
- It allows specifying the minimum log level
- It allows log file to be shared by multiple processes
- It allows changing character encoding used to write the text file

All the configuration of serilog comes with a default value so, you do not need specify all configuration value but specify the configuration value that you want to change from the default value.

Following code snippet specify minimum log level to warning, rolling interval to daily and output format:

```
.WriteTo.File(@"C:\logs\log.txt",
                    Serilog.Events.LogEventLevel.Warning,
                    rollingInterval: RollingInterval.Day,
                    outputTemplate: "{Timestamp:yyyy-MM-dd HH:mm:ss}
[{Level:u3}] {Message:lj}{NewLine}{Exception}")
```

Above code generate a new file every day and log with specified format (refer *Figure 8.4: File logging example using serilog)*:

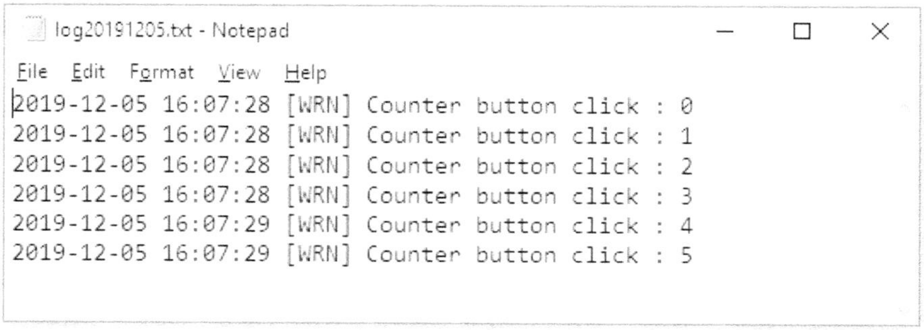

Figure 8.4: File logging example using serilog

Here, every file name ends with the day (date) as the rolling interval is set to daily. Similar way, serilog provides many other sinks that help you to write log in different platforms such as database and Seq.

Summary

- The exception is an unexpected error condition that generates due to logical error or technical error.

- Every unhandled exception considers as fatal to the circuit for the Blazor server app, and the Blazor app terminated circuit when an unhandled exception occurred.

- There are many places in the application where an exception can generate such as component instantiation and life cycle method, JavaScript interop, pre-rendering, and so on.

- The current version of Blazor does not provide costly exception handling, and it does not use the ASP.NET Core exception handling mechanism once circuit established. So, you must use a try-catch block to handle the exception.

- Blazor does not show error detail by default, but if you configured for detailed error, it displays a detailed error with cause and line number of exceptions.

- Logging the exception is an essential part as it helps you to debug code and investigate the problem in logic.

- These extensions are available for the Blazor app, and their implementation very similar to MEL (`Microsoft.Extensions.Logging`).

- The features of logging extension are very similar to MEL (`Microsoft.Extensions.Logging`).

- Blazor app also supports third-party logging providers such as serilog, elmah.io, and so on.

What you learned in this chapter?

In this chapter, you learned about how the Blazor app reacts to unhandled exception and what are different causes and places of the app where an exception can generate. You also learned about the logging extension supported by the Blazor app.

What next?

In the next chapter, you will be learned about how to create a single page application with the Blazor server project and how to do CRUD operation with EF code.

Questions

1. What is the behavior of the Blazor app when any unhandled exception occurred?

2. How can you handle the exception in the Blazor app?

3. Brief about the logging extension in the Blazor app?

CHAPTER 9

Getting Started with Blazor Using Visual Studio 2019

Introduction

The Blazor is a new web framework that can run in any browser. Using the Blazor framework, you can create a vibrant and modern **Single Page Application (SPA).** In previous chapters, you learned about the various features of the Blazor app. In this chapter, you will learn about how to create a SPA using Blazor and how to do **Create Read Update Delete (CRUD)** operations using entity framework core.

In this chapter, we'll cover the following topics

- Setting up the Blazor development environment using Visual Studio 2019
- Creating a single page application using Blazor
- Scaffolding the model using EF Core
- CRUD operation with EF in Blazor server app
- Installed project template for Blazor

Objective

- Understand how to setup development environment using VS 2019
- Understand how to do CRUD operation with EF in Blazor server app

Setting up the Blazor development environment using Visual Studio 2019

In *Chapter 1, An Introduction to Blazor,* you learned about how to set up a development environment. To start development using the Blazor framework, the .NET Core framework and IDE must be installed in your machine.

The Blazor introduced in .NET Core 3.0 so, .NET Core 3.0 or above version must install to start development Blazor app. As an IDE, either you can choose VS 2019 (or latest version) or VS Code. The VS 2019 is licensed IDE and available in Community / Professional / Enterprise editions. The VS Code is a free and cross-platform source code editor developed by Microsoft for Windows, Linux, and iOS. It provides almost all features that required for development, including integrations to source control (GitHub).

The current version of Blazor is only supporting the server app and provides a template for the server app. You can also install an additional template that use to create the Blazor app using CLI. After creating the Blazor app using an additional template, you can edit the app using VS 2019.

Creating a single page application using Blazor

The **single-page application (SPA)** is a website design approach where the new html page content is loaded into a pre-defined section of the page without re-render standard components such as header, footer, and so on. It means it rewrites page content without entire loading pages from a server. All modern framework such as Angular, Knockout, and so on, supports SPA. It helps to reduce the frequency of HTML, CSS, and script files loaded throughout the lifespan of the application.

There are some advantages of SPA like the SPA is fast as it loads resources such as JavaScript, CSS, and HTML once through the life of an application in the browser, and you can effectively use client-side features such as local storage. It also has some disadvantages, like it is challenging to make SEO optimization, JavaScript must present and enabled, and the SPA is less secure compared to the traditional application.

The default template of the Blazor app creates a single page application. When looking at the layout page of the default template, there are three sections: header, left panel, and body (refer *Figure 9.1: Map code snippet with output page*). The left panel contains the menu items, the header may contain the log and other information, and the body contains an HTML page (Blazor component). In SPA, all Blazor components are loaded to the body section. So, any new component is loaded into the body section, the header and left panel is not affected (not reload):

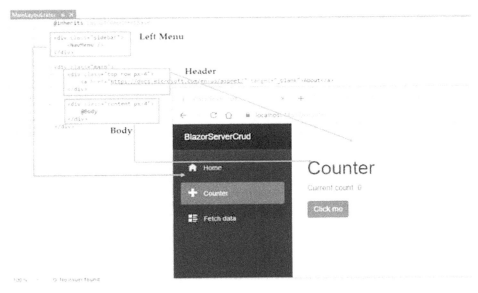

Figure 9.1: *Map code snippet with output page*

You can customize the layout based on your requirements. The Blazor routing mechanism always replaces the @Body directive with a new component. So, Blazor loads the component without refreshing the whole page.

Scaffolding the model using EF Core

The **entity framework (EF)** is a popular **object-relational mapper (ORM)** framework to work with the database. The EF core is lightweight, cross-platform, and extensible version of EF. The EF core provides database providers that use to access various databases such as SQL server, Cosmos, PostgreSQL, MySQL, Oracle DB, and so on. In ORM, data access is performed by the model. The model is a map with the database table, and the model's properties are mapped with the table's columns. The EF contains the context object that responsible for maintaining the session with a database; that is, it allows to query and saves data to the database using providers. You can also generate a model from an existing database using the EF migration command-line tool.

The EF core is not part of .NET Core framework as it has multiple providers so, you need to install the EF core database provider. You can install database providers using NuGet package manager or .NET Core CLI. Using the following command, you can install SQL server EF core database provider using the NuGet package manager.

```
PM> Install-Package Microsoft.EntityFrameworkCore.SqlServer
```

EF core also supports database migration. The migration is a database schema update that syncs with model changes during the development. The EF migration provides a way to update the database schema incrementally without losing the data. The migration is done using **command-line tools (CLI)** and API.

You can migrate using CLI, either package manager console tools or .NET Core CLI tools. Using the following command, you can install the .NET Core CLI tool for migration at the global level:

```
> dotnet tool install --global dotnet-ef
```

```
Administrator: Command Prompt

C:\>dotnet tool install --global dotnet-ef
You can invoke the tool using the following command: dotnet-ef
Tool 'dotnet-ef' (version '3.1.0') was successfully installed.
```

Figure 9.2: Install EF migration tool using .net core CLI

Apart from this, you need to install .NET Core framework SDK and `Install-Package Microsoft.EntityFrameworkCore.Design` for your project. You can install this package using the following command from the NuGet packages manager console:

```
PM> Install-Package Microsoft.EntityFrameworkCore.Design -Version 3.1.0
```

Using the following command, you can add initial migration. This command is looking for your project file so, it must in the root of the project file location:

```
> dotnet ef migrations add InitialCreate
```

This command generates two files to your project under the `Migrations` folders:

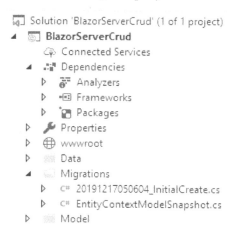

Figure 9.3: Create the initial migration

Following are the files generated:

- `Xxxxxxxxxxxxxxx_InitialCreate.cs`: It is the main migration file that contains a necessary command for upgrade and downgrade the database.
- `EntityContextModelSnapshot.cs`: This is a migration snapshot of the current model that helps to determine the changes that add to the next migration.

Using the following CLI command, you can apply the migration to the database:

```
> dotnet ef database update
```

You can remove the last applied migration using the following CLI command:

```
> dotnet ef migrations remove
```

The migration files generate based on the timestamp that helps you analyze changes in the model. You can also do the manual migration for the critical production site. The migration generates a script that does not affect the data.

CRUD operation with EF in Blazor server app

In *Chapter 1, An Introduction to Blazor*, you learned about how to create the Blazor server using VS 2019. To start the CRUD operation example, you need to create the Blazor server app. Following is the step by step procedure with detail explanation. The CRUD operation in the Blazor server app is the same as what you in the ASP. NET Core app.

1. Create `model`: The model looks like POCO. You can use `DataAnnotation` to define validation. There is schema related `DataAnnotation` also provided, such as `Table, Key`, and so on. The `DatabaseGenerated DataAnnotation` used to specify property behavior when generates the database column:

```
Namespace BlazorServerCrud.Model
{
    using System.ComponentModel.DataAnnotations;
    using System.ComponentModel.DataAnnotations.Schema;

    [Table("Customer")]
    public class Customer
    {
        [Key]
        [DatabaseGenerated(DatabaseGeneratedOption.Identity)]
```

```
        public int Id { get; set; }
        [StringLength(50)]
        [Required]
        public string Name { get; set; }
        [StringLength(50)]
        public string AddressLine1 { get; set; }
        [StringLength(50)]
        public string AddressLine2 { get; set; }
        [StringLength(50)]
        [Required]
        public string City { get; set; }
        [StringLength(50)]
        [Required]
        public string State { get; set; }
    }
}
```

Following is the equivalent Table schema (SQL script) of the model defined in the preceding step:

```
CREATE TABLE [dbo].[Customer](
        [Id] [int] IDENTITY(1,1) NOT NULL,
        [Name] [varchar](50) NULL,
        [AddressLine1] [varchar](50) NULL,
        [AddressLine2] [varchar](50) NULL,
        [City] [varchar](50) NULL,
        [State] [varchar](50) NULL,
 CONSTRAINT [PK_Customer] PRIMARY KEY CLUSTERED
(
        [Id] ASC
)WITH (PAD_INDEX = OFF, STATISTICS_NORECOMPUTE = OFF, IGNORE_DUP_
KEY = OFF, ALLOW_ROW_LOCKS = ON, ALLOW_PAGE_LOCKS = ON) ON [PRI-
MARY]
) ON [PRIMARY]
```

2. Create a `context` class: The `DbContext` class instance represents the session with the database, and it is used to querying and save data to the database.

In the following code, the entity context class has two constructors: one with parameter and another **without** parameter. The **without** parameter construction is used for migration. Here, you need to pass the hard code connection string. The Parameterized constructor takes connection string as a parameter. The context class contains all entities instance as **DbSet** property that is used to query and save the data in the database:

```
Namespace BlazorServerCrud.Model
{
    using Microsoft.EntityFrameworkCore;

    public class EntityContext : DbContext
    {
        string _connectionSting;
        public EntityContext(string connectionString)
        {
            _connectionSting = connectionString;
        }
        public virtual DbSet<Customer> Customer { get; set; }

        protected override void OnConfiguring(DbContextOptions-
Builder optionsBuilder)
        {
            if (!optionsBuilder.IsConfigured)
            {
                optionsBuilder.UseSqlServer(_connectionSting);
            }
        }
    }
}
```

3. Create a **Service** class: In this following example, CRUD operation related methods are created, such as:
   - **GetAll**: It returns all customers list from the database
   - **GetDetail**: It returns customer details based on the provided identity
   - **Add**: It adds a new customer
   - **Update**: It updates the details of existing customers

- **Delete**: It deletes the existing customer.

In the service class, you can also add business logic related methods that help you to validate the business scenario. In the following example, service class has parameterized constructor with connection string as parameter to initialize DBContext:

```
Namespace BlazorServerCrud.Data
{
    using BlazorServerCrud.Model;
    using Microsoft.EntityFrameworkCore;
    using System.Collections.Generic;
    using System.Threading.Tasks;
    public class CustomerService
    {
        EntityContext context;
        public CustomerService(string connectionString)
        {
            context = new EntityContext(connectionString);
        }

        //Get All
        public Task<List<Customer>> GetAll()
        {
            return context.Customer.ToListAsync();
        }

        //Get the details
        public Customer GetDetail(int id)
        {
            Customer customer = context.Customer.Find(id);
            return customer;
        }

        //Add new
```

```
    public void Add(Customer customer)
    {
        context.Customer.Add(customer);
        context.SaveChanges();
    }

    //Update
    public void Update(Customer customer)
    {
        context.Entry(customer).State = EntityState.Modified;
        context.SaveChanges();
    }

    //Delete
    public void Delete(int id)
    {
        Customer emp = context.Customer.Find(id);
        context.Customer.Remove(emp);
        context.SaveChanges();
    }
  }
}
```

4. Register the service in the **ConfigureService** method of **Startup** class (refer to the following code). The service class's constructor has a parameter that is defined in the connection string section of **appsettings.json**:

```
public void ConfigureServices(IserviceCollection services)
{
    services.AddRazorPages();
    services.AddSingleton<CustomerService>(new CustomerService(-
Configuration.GetConnectionString("default")));
    services.AddServerSideBlazor()
        .AddCircuitOptions(options => { options.DetailedErrors =
true; });

}
```

5. Create a list page: To create a list page, you need to inject the customer service created in the preceding section. The customer service's `GetAll` method returns all the customers. In following code, the customers list down using table structure and last column of table contains icon for edit and delete. On top of table, there is **Add customer** button for adding new customer:

```
@page "/fetchdata"


@using BlazorServerCrud.Data
@using BlazorServerCrud.Model


@inject CustomerService


<h1>Customer Master</h1>



@if (customers == null)
{
    <p><em>Loading...</em></p>
}
else
{
    <div style="padding-bottom:10px;">
        <a class="btn btn-info" href="/customers/0">Add Customer</a>
    </div>
    <table class="table">
        <thead>
            <tr>
                <th>Id</th>
                <th>Name</th>
                <th>Address Line 1</th>
                <th>Address Line 2</th>
                <th>City</th>
                <th>State</th>
```

```
                    <th></th>
                </tr>
            </thead>
            <tbody>
                @foreach (var customer in customers)
                {
                    <tr>
                        <td>@customer.Id</td>
                        <td>@customer.Name</td>
                        <td>@customer.AddressLine1</td>
                        <td>@customer.AddressLine2</td>
                        <td>@customer.City</td>
                        <td>@customer.State</td>
                        <td>
                            <a class="btn btn-info" href="/custom-
ers/@customer.Id">Edit</a>
                            <span style="padding-left:10px;"></span>
                            <button class="btn btn-danger">Delete</
button>
                        </td>
                    </tr>
                }
            </tbody>
        </table>
}

@code {
    List<Customer> customers;
    protected override async Task OnInitializedAsync()
    {
        await BindCustomer();
    }

    private async Task BindCustomer()
```

```
        {
            customers = await customerService.GetAll();
        }


    }
```

When you run the preceding code, it generates the following output (*Figure 9.4: Example - Customer List page*):

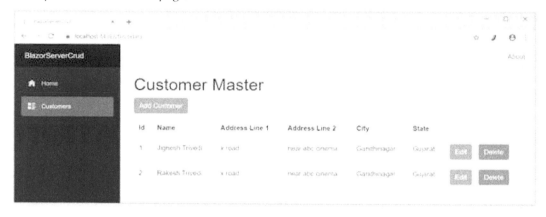

Figure 9.4: Example - Customer List page

Create Add/Edit page with validation

In *Chapter 3, Blazor Concepts*, you learned about the databinding and form validation in the Blazor app. Blazor app supports both one-way binding and two-way binding. The two-way binding allows you to bind the value of the variables/properties to the HTML element in DOM and vice-versa. The form is defined using the `EditForm` component in the Blazor app. Blazor app provides two components to show validation message: `ValidationSummary` component and `ValidationMessage` component. The `ValidationSummary` component used to summaries all the forms validation message and `ValidationMessage` component is used to display validation messages for a specific field. The Blazor form is also provided `OnValidSubmit` event that triggered when the form successfully submits and `OnInvalidSubmit` event when the form has validation error on submit.

The following code uses the `ValidationSummary` component to summaries all the forms of validation message and `OnValidSubmit` event to save valid data into the database. Here, Add or Edit customers identified by the value of the `CustomerId` parameter. If it is zero (0), then the page is for add a new customer else page is to update the existing component.

In edit customer page, existing customer information is retrieved in the `OnInitializedAsync` page life cycle method. The Add method of customer service is called when a page is in add mode else Update method is called in `HandleValidSubmit` event. After successfully insert or update customer record, it navigates to customer list page:

```
@page "/customers/{customerId:int}"

@using BlazorServerCrud.Data

@using BlazorServerCrud.Model


@inject CustomerService customerService

@inject NavigationManager NavigationManager


<h3>@(CustomerId == 0 ? "Add" : "Edit") Customer</h3>


<EditForm Model="@customer" OnValidSubmit="@HandleValidSubmit">

    <DataAnnotationsValidator />

    <div class="row content">

        <div class="col-md-2"><label for="name">Name*</label></div>

        <div class="col-md-3"><InputText id="name" @bind-Value="@customer.Name" /></div>

    </div>

    <div class="row content">

        <div class="col-md-2"><label for="addressLine1">Address Line 1</label></div>

        <div class="col-md-3"><InputText id="addressLine1" @bind-Value="@customer.AddressLine1" /></div>

    </div>

    <div class="row content">

        <div class="col-md-2"><label for="addressLine2">Address Line 2</label></div>

        <div class="col-md-3"><InputText id="addressLine2" @bind-Value="@customer.AddressLine2" /></div>

    </div>

    <div class="row content">

        <div class="col-md-2"><label for="city">City*</label></div>
```

```
        <div class="col-md-1"><InputText id="city" @bind-Value="@custom-
er.City" /></div>
    </div>
    <div class="row content">
        <div class="col-md-2"><label for="state">State*</label></div>
        <div class="col-md-1"><InputText id="state" @bind-Value="@cus-
tomer.State" /></div>
    </div>
    <div class="row content">
        <button class="btn btn-info" type="submit">Save</button>
    </div>
    <br />
    <div class="row">
        <ValidationSummary />
    </div>


</EditForm>

@code {
    [Parameter]
    public int CustomerId { get; set; }
    Customer customer;
    protected override async Task OnInitializedAsync()
    {
        if (CustomerId > 0)
        {
            customer = customerService.GetDetail(CustomerId);
        }
        else
        {
            customer = new Customer();
        }
    }
    private void HandleValidSubmit()
```

```
    {
        SaveCustomer();
    }
    private void SaveCustomer()
    {
        if (CustomerId == 0)
        {
            customerService.Add(customer);
        }
        else
        {
            customerService.Update(customer);
        }
        NavigationManager.NavigateTo("fetchdata");
    }
}
```

The **Add customer** page looks like as following *Figure 9.5: Example – Add Customer page:*

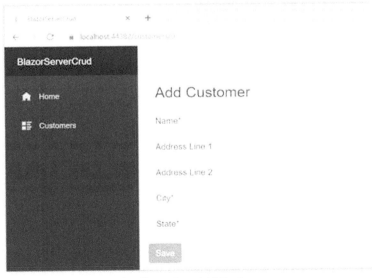

Figure 9.5: Example – Add Customer page

When you press the **Save** button, the Blazor engine will perform the validation defined using DataAnnotation. If anything is invalid in form, it shows message in summary (refer *Figure 9.6: Example – Add Customer with validation messages*):

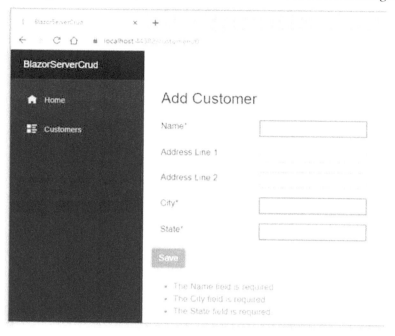

Figure 9.6: Example – Add Customer with validation messages

The validation works similarly in add and edits the customer page. In the case of multiple validations defined on the model's property, the Blazor engine performs the validation one by one and stops validating property when the first invalid instance found. For example, Name property contains two validation `Required` and `StringLength`. When the **Name** filed is empty, required validation fired but not string length.

Delete customer

Delete customer functionality is quite easy to implement. You need to pass customer ID (that you want to delete) to the customer service's `Delete` method. The record permanently removes from the database in delete functionality so, you may want to ask for confirmation about whether the user sure to delete the record or not.

The Blazor does not provide a built-in component to display confirmation. You can use the Bootstrap model component or JavaScript 's confirm box in this case. To invoke these options, you can use JavaScript interop.

The idea is when a user clicks on the delete button, the customer id temporary stored and JavaScript method calls to show confirmation. Once a user confirms delete, the C# method is called from JavaScript to delete records.

In the following code, the component instance is passed to JavaScript using the OnAfterRender life cycle event, and the ConfirmDelete method called when a user clicks on the **Delete** button. In this method, customerId is temporarily stored in the variable and call the confirmDelete of JavaScript:

```
@page "/fetchdata"


...

...


@inject IJSRuntime JsRuntime;


<h1>Customer Master</h1>



@if (customers == null)
{
    <p><em>Loading...</em></p>
}
else
{
    ...

    ...

    ...

    <table class="table">
        <thead>
            <tr>
                ...

                ...

                ...

            </tr>
        </thead>
```

```
        <tbody>
            @foreach (var customer in customers)
            {
                <tr>
                    ...
                    ...
                    ...
                    <td>
                        <a class="btn btn-info" href="/customers/@cus-
tomer.Id">Edit</a>
                        <span style="padding-left:10px;"></span>
                        <button class="btn btn-danger" @onclick="@(() =>
ConfirmDelete(customer.Id) )">Delete</button>
                    </td>
                </tr>
            }
        </tbody>
    </table>
}


@code {
    ...
    ...
    ...
    protected override void OnAfterRender(bool firstRender)
    {
        if (firstRender)
        {
            JsRuntime.InvokeAsync<object>("passInstanceToJS", DotNetOb-
jectReference.Create(this));
        }
    }


    protected void ConfirmDelete(int id)
```

```
    {
        DeleteId = id;
        JsRuntime.InvokeAsync<int>("confirmDelete");
    }


    [JSInvokable]
    public bool DeleteCustomer(bool confirmed)
    {
        if (confirmed)
        {
            customerService.Delete(DeleteId);
            return true;
        }
        return false;
    }
}
```

The JavaScript method looks like the following code. It asks for confirm delete and call `DeleteCustomer` method (C#) if a user confirms for delete:

```
function confirmDelete() {
    var r = confirm("Are you sure you want to delete Customer");
    myClsObj.invokeMethodAsync("DeleteCustomer", r)
        .then(data => {
            if (data) {
                window.location.reload();
            }
        });
}


var myClsObj;
function passInstanceToJS(instance) {
    myClsObj = instance;
}
```

This code shows JavaScript 's confirm box when you click on the **Delete** button (refer *Figure 9.7: Example – Delete Customer confirm box):*

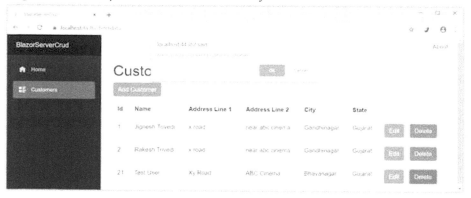

Figure 9.7: *Example – Delete Customer confirm box*

Once the deleted customer gets deleted, function pointer return to JavaScript function's **then** block. Here, you may reload the page so, updated customer data can be available in the table.

Installed project template for Blazor

The default template to create the Blazor server app is provided with the .NET Core framework 3.0. You can also install templates from the Visual Studio marketplace. To install the project templates, go to **Extensions | Manage Extensions.** It lists down all available temples in the Visual Studio marketplace. You can also search required template and then download it (refer *Figure 9.8: Install third party project template):*

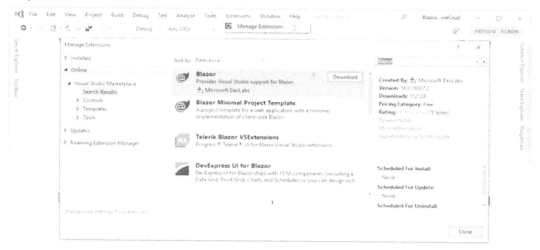

Figure 9.8: *Install third party project template*

When you select any available template, it shows template related information such as author, version, no of downloads, release note, and so on.

You can also create own project template using the VSIX project template and uploaded it to the Visual Studio market; hence it available to another person for use. Once the project template is installed, the project template listed in the **New Project** dialog (**File | New | Project)** in VS 2019.

Summary

- You can use Visual Studio 2019 or Visual Studio Code as IDE to develop Blazor application
- You can also create/Build/run Blazor application using .NET Core CLI; however, it required a template to be install
- The default template of Blazor app creates single page application
- To develop a data access layer in Blazor app, you can use any ORM such as entity framework core
- Entity framework core supports database migration
- You can migrate using CLI either package manager console tools or .NET Core CLI tools
- You can use the third party project template to create Blazor app

What you learned in this chapter?

Up to this chapter, you learned about the various concept of the Blazor app and how you can use this concept in various scenarios. In this chapter, you learn how to create an end to end application using the Blazor server app project template with EF core and also learned how to install the third party project template.

What next?

In the next chapter, you will be learned about the various hosting models that can use to deploy the Blazor server app, such as IIS and Azure.

Questions

1. Brief about how to create the Blazor server app using VS 2019?
2. Brief about the EF core migration process?
3. How to install a third party project template in VS 2019?

Chapter 10

Hosting
and
Deployment

Introduction

In previous chapters, you learned about the various features of the Blazor server app that required to develop business applications. The next step is to deploy the application so that it is available for use. There are multiple options to deploy Blazor server app such as deploy on IIS, Azure, and so on. In this chapter, you will learn how to deploy the Blazor server app on IIS and Azure.

In this chapter, we'll cover the following topics

- Publish Blazor App
- Deploying Blazor app on IIS
- Deploying Blazor app on Azure

Objective

Understand the hosting and deployment model of the Blazor server app and learn how to deploy an app on IIS and Azure.

Publish Blazor server app

To deploy the application, the first step is to publish an application. When you publish an application, all application files compiled into the assembly (dll) and copied to the specified location. The project dependencies and static files are also copied in the same folder. The views are also compiled in the project assembly file.

The Blazor use ASP.NET Core publishing and hosting model so you can publish Blazor application using VS 2019 editor and .NET Core CLI.

To publish the Blazor server app, right-click on the project, and click **Publish** option from the context menu (refer *Figure 10.1: Create a profile - Publish option in VS 2019*). Now it asks for the publish options. There are multiple publish the target available such as AppService, Azure virtual machine FTP, Folder, and so on. You can select the **Folder** option to generate publish build on the local machine. Your selection of publishing target stored as **Profile** in the Visual Studio:

Figure 10.1: Create a profile - Publish option in VS 2019

Once the profile is created in visual studio, it can be used for the next time when publishing the application. After storing the profile, the **Publish** button available (refer *Figure 10.2: Publish Blazor server app):*

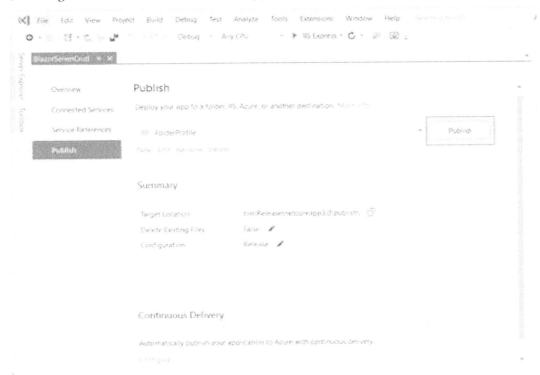

Figure 10.2: Publish Blazor server app

Once the application publishes successfully, it is ready to host. You can also configure for **Continuous Integration and Continuous Delivery (CICD).**

Alternatively, you can publish the Blazor app using .NET Core CLI. The dotnet publish command generates the application deployment files and their dependency into the specified folder. You can also define configuration parameters with this command, such as configuration (debug/release), framework, manifest file, output directory, and so on.

Deploying Blazor app on IIS

The Blazor server uses the same hosting model as ASP.NET Core used so, deployment of the Blazor app on IIS is very similar to deploy the ASP.NET Core app on IIS. It executes server from ASP.NET core app and UI handling (UI update and event handing) is managed using the SignalR.

Prerequisites

The following are prerequisites that need to install before starting to deploy the Blazor app on IIS. Before installing these prerequisites, IIS must properly configure:

- .NET Core Runtime
- Hosting Bundle Installer

These prerequisites are download from **https://dotnet.microsoft.com/download** (refer *Figure 10.3: Download prerequisites*):

Figure 10.3: *Download prerequisites*

For .NET Core runtime, Both 64 / 32-bit download options are available. On the same page, you can download **Hosting Bundle Installer** (refer *Figure 10.4: Download prerequisites: .net core runtime and hosting bundle*):

Figure 10.4: *Download prerequisites: .net core runtime and hosting bundle*

It is recommended to install the latest version of .NET Core runtime and hosting bundle. The host bundle must install after the successful installation of .NET Core runtime. It is recommended to restart the machine after installing all prerequisites.

Configure IIS

Once both prerequisites installed, you can start the configure IIS. Following are the steps to configure IIS:

1. Add Website on IIS. To add a new website, right-click on **Sites**, and select **Add Website** option in the following screenshot:

Figure 10.5: Add new web site in IIS

It will open a window where you can do the configuration for your website, such as site name, application pool, IP address/port, the path of application build, and so on. (refer *Figure 10.6: IIS – Add Website configuration*):

Figure 10.6: IIS – Add Website configuration

2. Configure the application pool. In preceding step, the **Edit Application Pool** selected to run the Blazor app. Go to **Edit Application Pool** and double click on application pool so, it opens in **Edit** mode (refer *Figure 10.7: IIS – Manage Application pool*):

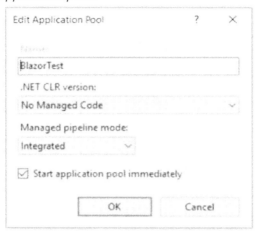

Figure 10.7: *IIS – Manage Application pool*

The ASP.NET Core does not use .NET CLR, so; you need to select **No Managed Code** from **.NET CLR version dropdown.** The IIS use AspNetCoreModuleV2 to host Blazor application (refer *Figure 10.8: IIS – AspNetCoreModuleV2*):

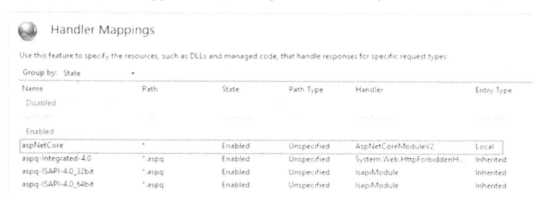

Figure 10.8: *IIS – AspNetCoreModuleV2*

In this way, you can deploy Blazor application on IIS on windows operating system. The VS 2019 also provides an option that allows you to configure IIS and push application build using web deploy or file transfer.

Deploying Blazor app on Azure

There are multiple ways to host applications on Azure, such as host application as static content, host as App service, and so on. The VS 2019 allows hosting applications on Azure as **App Service** and App service Linux. The VS2019 also provides an option to host applications on Azure Virtual machines.

Prerequisites

To host an application on Azure as App service, you must have an Azure subscription account. If you haven't an Azure subscription account, you can create a free Azure account. It is only the prerequisites to host a Blazor application on Azure.

Deploy app on Azure as app service

The following are the steps to host an application on Azure as App service.

Create publish profile with create app service or selecting existing one

The VS2019 provides an option that enables you to host application in-app service from the published app. To publish the Blazor server app, right-click on the project, and click publish option from the context menu (refer *Figure 10.1: Create a profile - Publish option in VS 2019*). It Provides the various options for publishing; one of them is **App Service** (refer *Figure 10.9: Publish App in Azure app service*):

Figure 10.9: Publish App in Azure app service

You can either create a new **App Service** or select the existing one. By clicking of **Create Profile** button, VS 2019 will create a profile that host application on **Azure App** Service.

Sign in using Azure account

Now, you need to sign-in with Azure account. If you did not have an Azure account, you could create a free account. To sign-in with existing Azure account, click **Sign In** link (refer *Figure 10.10: Create new App Service*):

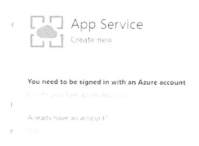

Figure 10.10: Create new App Service

Configure App Service.

When you click on **Sign In** link, it will ask Azure account credentials. After a successful login, it allows you to configure App Service (refer *Figure 10.11: Create New App service- Add configuration*):

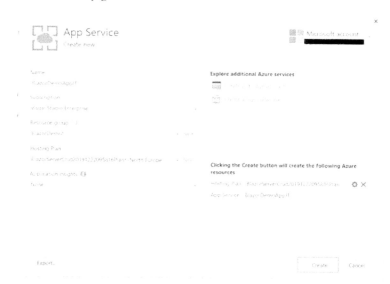

Figure 10.11: Create New App service- Add configuration

Here, you can configure the following items of App Service:

- **Name**: Name of the App Service. The name of App Service is unique across the world. The URL of your site is {App Service name}.azurewebsites. net.

- **Subscription**: Select the subscription that used for this App service. The subscription is used for billing purposes.

- **Resource Group**: You can either create and select a new resource group or select an existing resource group.

- **Hosting Plan:** you can either select the existing plan or create and select a new plan for App Service.

- **Application Insights:** Application Insights is used to monitor live application in terms of performance anomalies. If you do not want any kind of monitoring of service, select **none** from the dropdown list.

Now, click on **Create** button to create **App Service** and save created profile in VS2019. It takes a few minutes to deploy **App Service** on Azure Portal. The time for deploying App service depends on your internet connection speed.

Once **App Service** created successfully, the **Publish** button is available (refer *Figure 10.12: Publish app on Azure App Service*). Here, it also shows a summary of your configuration such URL, resource group, target framework, and so on:

Figure 10.12: *Publish app on Azure App Service*

Publish application on app service

Click on the **Publish** button to publish the application as an **App Service** on Azure Portal. After successfully, publish the application on Azure, the website automatically launches to default browser (refer *Figure 10.13: Run application from Azure portal):*

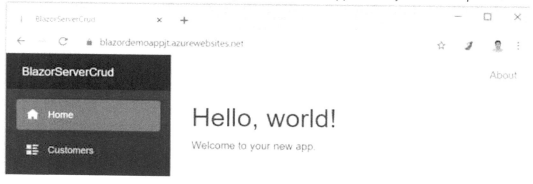

Figure 10.13: Run application from Azure portal

You can also edit the configuration **App Service** from Azure Portal. The **App Service** created from publishing option is available on Azure Portal (refer *Figure 10.14: App service located on Azure portal):*

Figure 10.14: App service located on the Azure portal

When you hosted an application in **App Services**, your database must be online; otherwise, your application cannot able to access the database. There are many security concerns when your database is online. You can use the SQL service provided by Azure. The advantage of use SQL service is security concerns taken care of by Azure.

Create database server and database on Azure

You can create an SQL server and database using Azure Portal. The followings are the step to create a DB server and SQL DB on Azure.

Login to Azure portal and select SQL databases from the left menu

To create SQL DB, first, log in to Azure Portal and select **SQL databases** from the left menu. Now click on **Add** to add new database (refer *Figure 10.15: Azure Portal - Add SQL database):*

Figure 10.15: Azure Portal - Add SQL database

Next step is to fill-up required information to create SQL database (refer *Figure 10.16: Azure Portal - Configure SQL server database):*

Figure 10.16: Azure Portal - Configure SQL server database

Following information need to fill-up to create a new SQL database:

- **Subscription**: Select the subscription that used for the SQL database. The subscription is used for billing purposes
- **Resource group**: You can either create and select a new resource group or select the existing resource group
- **Database name:** Name of the database
- **Server:** You can use the existing database server or create a new server
- **Want to use SQL elastic pool?:** It provides a solution for performance management using multiple database usage. It is a cost-effective solution
- **Compute + storage:** This is the SQL server configuration tire. The default configuration is two vCores with 32 GB of HDD

To create a SQL database, you can use either select existing server or create a new server. You can create a new SQL server from **Create SQL Database** screen (refer *Figure 10.16: Azure Portal - Configure SQL server database*). To create a new SQL server, click **Create new** link of **server** label (refer *Figure 10.17: Azure Portal - Add new SQL server*):

Figure 10.17: Azure Portal - Add new SQL server

Following information need to fill-up to create new SQL Server on Azure Portal:

- **Server name**: name of the SQL server
- **Server admin login:** SQL server admin user name

- **Password**: admin user password
- **Confirm Password**: confirm admin password
- **Location**: location of SQL server

When you click on the **OK** button, Azure will create the SQL server, and it available to use to create SQL database after server deployment.

Create a database

When you click on **Review + Create** button of **Create SQL Database** screen (*Figure 10.16: Azure Portal - Configure SQL server database*), database information that you have fill-up in previously is available for review (refer *Figure 10.18: Azure Portal - Create SQL server database*) and click on **Create** button, Azure will create SQL database on specified server:

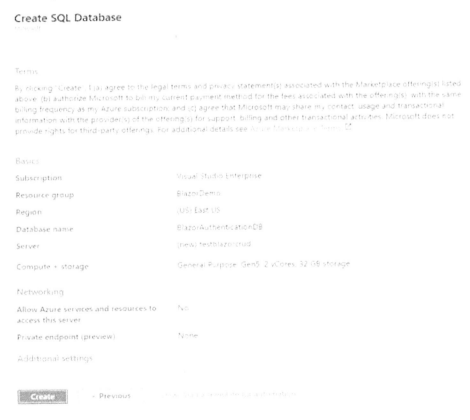

Figure 10.18: Azure Portal - Create a SQL server database

You can modify the SQL database information when clicking on the **Previous** button.

Get connection string

After creating the SQL database, you need a connection string to access this SQL database from your application.

To get connection string, click **SQL Server** and then click **Connection strings** menu under the **Settings** menu (refer *Figure 10.19: Azure Portal - SQL server Connection string*). This connection string is replaced with default connection mention in `appSettings.json` in Blazor app:

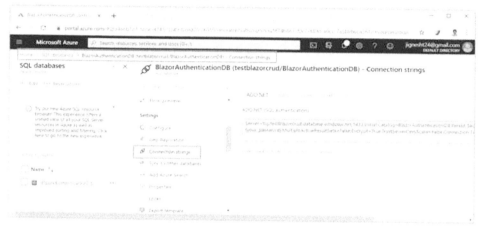

Figure 10.19: *Azure Portal - SQL server Connection string*

Configure firewall for SQL server

The next step is to configure a firewall. You can create firewall rules that allow the client IP address to access the Azure SQL server.

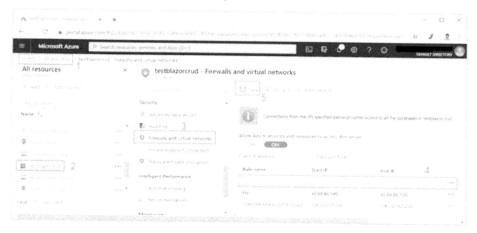

Figure 10.20: *Azure Portal - Configure firewall for SQL server*

To configure a firewall, select SQL server, and select `Firewalls and virtual networks` under the `Security` menu. The firewall rules allow you to specify the client IP address that can be allowed to access and click on the `Save` button to save new firewall rule:

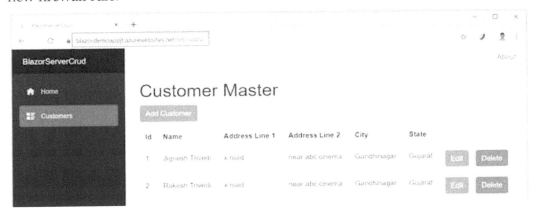

Figure 10.21: Azure Portal – Retrieve data from Azure SQL database

Once the SQL server and database configured, you can access the database from your application. Still, your client IP address must specify in firewall rule (refer *Figure 10.21: Azure Portal – Retrieve data from Azure SQL database*).

Summary

- You can publish Blazor server app using VS 2019 or .NET Core CLI
- There are multiple publish targets available such as AppService, Azure virtual machine FTP, Folder, and so on.
- The .NET Core Runtime and Hosting Bundle installer need to install to deploy Blazor app on IIS.
- The ASP.NET core does not use .NET CLR so; you need to select `No Managed Code` from `.NET CLR version` dropdown when creating an application pool
- You can deploy the Blazor server app on Azure using the VS2019 publish option by selecting `App Service.`
- You must have Azure subscription to deploy the application on Azure.
- You can also host your SQL database on Azure.

What you learned in this chapter?

In this chapter, you learned about how to host a Blazor server application on the IIS and Azure App service and also learned how to configure SQL Server on Azure using portal.

Questions

1. What are prerequisites need to install to deploy the Blazor app on IIS?
2. Explain steps to host the Blazor app on IIS?
3. What are the prerequisites required to deploy an application on Azure?
4. Explain steps to host the Blazor app on Azure?
5. Explain steps to deploy the SQL database on Azure?

Lightning Source UK Ltd.
Milton Keynes UK
UKHW050700260722
406393UK00006B/943

9 789389 845464